Give Him what he cannot give to himself

Touch his heart

Betty Amiina

BALBOA
PRESS

A DIVISION OF HAY HOUSE

Balboa Press books may be ordered through booksellers or by contacting:

Balboa Press
A Division of Hay House
1663 Liberty Drive
Bloomington, IN 47403
www.balboapress.com
1 (877) 407-4847

Because of the dynamic nature of the Internet, any web addresses or links contained in this book may have changed since publication and may no longer be valid. The views expressed in this work are solely those of the author and do not necessarily reflect the views of the publisher, and the publisher hereby disclaims any responsibility for them.

The author of this book does not dispense medical advice or prescribe the use of any technique as a form of treatment for physical, emotional, or medical problems without the advice of a physician, either directly or indirectly. The intent of the author is only to offer information of a general nature to help you in your quest for emotional and spiritual well-being. In the event you use any of the information in this book for yourself, which is your constitutional right, the author and the publisher assume no responsibility for your actions.

Any people depicted in stock imagery provided by Thinkstock are models,
and such images are being used for illustrative purposes only.
Certain stock imagery © Thinkstock.

Print information available on the last page.

ISBN: 978-1-5043-4441-8 (sc)
ISBN: 978-1-5043-5224-6 (e)

Balboa Press rev. date: 07/13/2016

It's true that our God is Iam That Iam. He can be anything, and He can do all things but what I know He cannot praise Himself and He cannot worship Him self. It is impossible for Him to do, and that is why He created us in His image. God made us to worship Him, Isaiah 43:21 says, this people I have formed for my self shall declare my praise. John 23:4 we see that He seeks for the true worshippers to worship Him. What else can you give Him? He owns the whole universe, can you build a home for Him? There is no home here that can contain Him heaven is His throne and the whole earth is His foot stool but if you want to invite Him into your heart He is gentle and humble enough to make it His home. God does not eat our food the only food He eats and the only drink He drinks is our worship. God yearns for our praises imagine someone being so thirst and nobody gives him a drink. Why did God love David so much? He a man after His heart! No wonder he had victory over his enemies you can't feed God and be defeated, impossible. I once asked 6 years old son that why does he worship God and he said so He can jump and dance. If it is true that God dances, then chains will brake, so if I were you I would praise Him now. May be we cannot be like David but we can give Him our best. Imagine If God looks down from heaven and finds you!

You can also touch His, so praise Him as you read this book. You may be on train going to work or on a bus or even in KFC and you feel like you want to tell God something beautiful, just get your book and read it.

Thank you for praising our Big God.

INTRODUCTION

God Almighty, Majesty, King of Kings, and Lord of Lords, Ancient of days, The Great I am. I am that I am, King of Glory, Lord of Host, consuming fire, Loving Father, Saviour, Redeemer Lion of Judah, Prince of Peace, Jesus I worship you.

God of everything, creator of heaven and earth, Adonai, Elohim, Elushadai, Mighty to save, mighty in battle, Glorious King, Secret place, mighty God, Alpha and Omega.

I salute you.

My helper, My strong tower, My hiding place my beautiful place, my hope, my healer, my fighter, my deliverer, my hedge of fire, my defender, my warrior, my teacher, my revealer, God I praise your holy name.

Rose of Sharon, lily of the Valley, Invisible God. Beautiful morning star, husband to the widows, father of orphans, mother of motherless, Director, Father Glory be to your name.

You are full of wonders, you are full of surprises, blessed be your Holy name, oh Lord, I lift you higher.

I praise and adore you, I thank you oh Lord, I glorify you, you are worthy, and glorious are your works.

God of wonders heaven and earth adore you, angels bow before you. Babies sing for you most beautiful.

You are awesome, you are seated in the class of your own, you have no age mate, none can be compared to you, and none can be equal to you.

You are God and you are God alone, all power belongs to you, you do impossible; you are not a liar oh God. You are always on time. You are higher than heaven, bigger than the universe.

Sovereign God, you rule by power, everlasting Father, Jehovah Nissi Great Commander, patient God, caring Father, you have the whole world in your hand.

I thank you Lord, without you I am nothing, my help is in you, I will talk about your goodness, I will tell nations about your power, I call you Big and mighty because that is what you are.

Thank you for putting a new song in my mouth, and help me always to wake up singing a new song to you. I just can't thank you enough you are too wonderful to me you are always there for me, you seem to be very far Jesus, but I know you are near, you have fought my battles, you are so amazing, I will praise you forever.

When I see what you have done for me, and remember where you found me and know that you have not finished with me. I just want to jump up and praise your name. Though sometimes I don't know how to praise you, no matter how hard I try, Can I ever give you more praises than the blessings you shower on me every day?

Jesus, I can't count all my blessings they are too much for me to talk about, Where can I start? From healing or protection? What shall I ever give you! What is it that you don't have or what you cannot do? I will worship you because that is what you cannot do, and for this reason you created me.

I praise you, I worship you, you are too much in my life, When I look around me, I see reasons to praise you and to be grateful.

JESUS YOUR NAME IS AMEN

To be honest, I don't think I can write all songs that I have and finish in one book or even tell you the meaning!! Each song in this book talks about God's names, He has many names, and each name has a meaning, we know that names are so powerful. My elder sister in Uganda almost two years ago, was found with breast cancer.

I had actually seen her in a coffin because that was the plan of the enemy. One day I came from church and I went to sleep it was Sunday afternoon then I had dream, where she was in a coffin and I saw many people surrounding her. So when I woke up, I prayed and I told God that any plan of the enemy concerning her will not stand in the name of Jesus.

Four months later, I called her and she told me that she had cancer, and she did not want to tell me, she was going to have her breast removed. Wen she told me, I told her not worry Because the name of Jesus is higher than cancer.

I did not stop there I reminded her of her name, and I asked her if she really knows the meaning of her name. I told her that her name is hope, so I have hope that you will live but not die and I told her that if does not believe it, believe it.

God's name are call Him what you want Him to be. He is one God but each name is unique, you call that name when you need it, when I am hungry He is my provider.

Who can understand God and His names? I am getting excited here because there is one name that so highly exalted, Jesus, the name of Jesus is higher than all His names! He is God and Jesus is His name So if someone was to choose one name what will it be? I thought I could choose Man of war! Then what about Amen or what about love? Our God is love, it's love that brought Him into this world and its love that makes His hands to be open always waiting for any sinner that comes to Him.

One day my 6 year old son told me, Mummy love doesn't get angry but sometime you are angry and you teach me love!

No matter how much, I meditate on God's names, the name Amen seals everything, Amen Means so let it be, it is God's signature. SO since It is His signature, I know that whatever He said concerning me, no body has power to change it. He is the only one with a final say and no one can ask Him what He does, if He decides to visit me in the night who will meet Him and ask Him where He's coming from!

Jesus, I can't get enough of you, You are so amazing I have a reason to call you God because I have seen your power, what can I say, but to say thank you, There is nothing greater than saying thank you.

I thought I was nobody because I did not study much, I did not think that anything good will ever come out me. When I come to UK, I told my self that one day I will study hair dressing since did not become a nurse which was my dream when I was growing up. I thought I can still touch people because I love caring, but for some reasons I did not go to college. I started cleaning people's homes, but in 2011, I had a dream where I was cleaning then I a man came, he took the bloom from my hands, he threw it away and said, this is not want I want you to do. I kept on cleaning, but whenever to clean I would be sick, there were times that I could not bend at all because of back pain. In my heart I thought it's because I fell off the bus, I did not have a Doctor and my back was not treated. I stopped for a while, but because I needed money and I could not any other job because of restrictions at that time I went back. In 2013 December I joined a new church, life house, then one Sunday morning as l was sleeping, I heard voice, don't clean people's houses again. In that same dream I saw Pastor, he came and held my hands and walked me to the altar. He did not say anything to me, and when I saw I him, I did not tell him anything about the dream, I didn't want to talk about dreams again because of the bad experience I had in the old church. I just ignored the dream, I didn't think about it again, but one week later during evening worship, someone came and put his hands on me and said, God wants to sing for Him! When he said it, I said me! Some weeks later I went to church, after the service, a lady who is one of the elders in church stood front in case some people want further prayers, I went to greet her then she asked if I needed prayers I answered no I just wanted to greet her. She gave me Jeremiah 1:5 and told me that people will receive healing as I worship. When she told me in my heart I said, here is a spirit of God in this church because that was the verse came to my spirit early in the morning before I went to church, and it was the same verse that I had dreamt of when I was still in my old church.

I never knew I was born to sing for God, I have never trusted my voice, though He does not care about the voice but about the heart that someone has for Him. My mother told me when she was still alive, She looked at me and said that I will serve God, but I told her that I will not, and I remember gave her two reasons why I will not serve Him. Number one was, back home people who served God in our villages were really and poor and I wanted to be rich, I wanted to have a lot of money. Number two, I told her that when Jesus comes, I will go with her since she was born again. I remember one day she gathered us and said, my children, my children why don't you give your lives to Jesus but my answer was Mummy, your dress is very big, when Jesus comes I will hide inside it and go with you. She answered me, Betty, my child, in heaven I will go alone, a time came my mother passed away and she really went alone. When she passed, I was not at home with her, I was with my sister in town where she was working as a teacher. In 1995 August Saturday night I had a dream, I saw my mother going to church with one woman who happened to be our neighbour. On their way back home, they stopped somewhere, I can see the place not very far from home, that woman gave something to my mum and she ate it. After eating it they all went home, after that my mother said that she wanted to eat sweet corn I saw her going to the farm, she cut the corn, took it home and roasted it, and ate it.

After that I saw her laying in her bed, beside it there was a candle burning but in my heart I wondered if it will not fall on her, the whole room was full of light. She was alone in her room but out side the house in the compound and in living room were many people, some of them were eating and dancing, I wondered if there was a party going on.

Then at the end I saw my Mum, this time she, was sitting on a chair but really I can't explain it, I have never seen a chair like that, her dress was as white as snow, it was very long, in her hand was a long stick, may be I can call it the rod or the staff which Moses had and she had a crown on her head, it was so brilliant pure white which I have never seen. Every thing about her changed she looked so beautifully thought she was dark in complexion and she looked like she was eighteen year again!

After that she looked at me and smiled, she waved good bye and started going, when I saw her going, I started running after her, it's like I wanted to go with her but she kept on going on the other side there were people waiting for her when she reached gate the door opened then she entered.

But as I forced my to catch up with her, a big fence cough my legs and I fell down crying then I woke up. In the morning my sister prepared for church, she asked me if I wanted to go but I told her no, she tried to know why I was not going to church, but I didn't tell her anything, I asked my self, is my Mum dead! At that time I didn't how to rebuke a bad dream in the name of Jesus, even if I had to rebuke it, my mother was already dead and buried, I spent the whole day sad. My sister nearly caught me crying but when I saw her, I pretended that I was blowing my nose. The next day she went to work, at that time she was the head teacher and we lived in the school premises, so here office was not far from where we lived. As she was approaching her office, I saw a young man on a bicycle, he came and he handed a letter to her, immediately she opened it I was still watching, I don't think she even finished reading it. The next thing I saw she put hands on her head and started crying and she returned home and Betty Mum is dead and they buried her yesterday! She passed away on Saturday and on Sunday they buried her! My Father will explain how she died, because him and her women must have killed her that is why buried her quickly before I arrived, they knew I would cause trouble for them. How can they throw my mother like someone who have no children.? My asked angrily, then I said, Hope, I knew Mummy is gone, I saw every thing in a dream, I saw how she went to church with one woman and I saw her eating somethings, in my heart I wondered what will our Father tell us when he sees us. That same day went home, when we reached, some of our neighbours came to sympathise with us and others were still there. On the other hand my Father had turned the whole house upside-down, looking for the money that my mother my kept!!! He said, how come she wore one dress! So she must have left money some where, our stepmother and her two friends were there also when our Father saw my sister, he said, trouble maker has come! The first thing my sister asked our Father was, how did our mother died? And did you have to Bury her so first? Your mother had malaria, he answered, but my sister wanted more answers then she said she wanted post-mortem, but there was one man who asked us that, will post-mortem bring your mother back? Your mother has suffered enough, now let her rest God will judge.

I stayed in Uganda for a while, then one night I dreamt that I was in an aeroplane and a I heard a voice, you are going to London!!

I kept that dream to my self, did not tell anyone because it was too big for me, I said how could I ever go to London! Where would I get money to take me to take me there? But that very day my Auntie told me that she was preparing for me to come, when she told me, I looked back to where I was born and In my heart I said you mean I can go to England! And many people did not believe that I cam to England, the dream was to big for me, but not for God.

Nothing is impossible for Him when he is planning something for someone, He looks for somebody to use, that's why we are His extensions, some of us are the extension of His hands, while other are His legs and others can be His mouth.

Any way I came to UK, but I did not settle because it's not the country of my birth, I did not know I will meet traffic on my way, things were not moving the way I thought they Would be. Thought already in UK, I needed some things to be able to get something or to do something and devil came and stood in my way then my life turned out in away in never thought it would be.

But God was with me, if someone thinks that suffering can kill anyone, it's not true, If it was then I wouldn't be standing by now. I'm sure, it makes someone stronger and wiser, but the most important it brings one close to God.

Has anyone ever suffered to the point that all you wanted was just to die? Being in this country as cold as it's for almost two weeks, you don't know what you will eat or where you will sleep. At some point I wondered if I was a human being I wanted to die so I could rest from suffering but I couldn't.

I remember one night walking to the police station, I wanted to ask for help but then I thought they will just put me to plane and send me back to Uganda and I did not want to return to Uganda. Then I called my elder sister and told her that I was suffering was to much, but I did not tell her that I was outside. That night I slept out side a gas mitre place, it was concrete and very cold, and I was lucky that nobody came to check gas. God who protected me has a bigger plan for my life easier, at that time I was working at Matilda 's hair salon in shepherds bush training as a hair dresser. Those Ladies really took care of me, they give me food and bought African bread for me, I think that is why I like Ghanaians!

One night I was on the street in the middle of the night, I did not know what to do because I didn't have where to go. Then I saw street boys, and I thought if I could just go near them, then they will have a reason to kill me, but no one even touched me I felt disappointed.

After that I found where to sleep, I was very cold and hungry I don't known how I managed to sleep, as I was sleeping, I heard a man's voice, nobody will touch you! I did not doubt I knew it was God, and as soon as I woke up my phone rung was it uncle Sam, he asked me if I was okay, I told him yes. Then I started wondering around the street again, I went to Mac Donald's, washed my face and sat down I didn't have money to buy food I was just watching people eating breakfast, I desired to eat their left overs, but some of them would just finish everything. How big is breakfast! As I was sitting there, I was reminded about the poor man Lazarus who desired to eat crumbs that fell from the rich man's table Luke 16: 19-21. I thought about checking in the bin if may be I could find food but I was shy, then I said, it's better to be ashamed. Even as I am writing this book I am praising God because I know that day I ate from the bin, He saw me.

Another time I thought I could hang myself, I took a scarf and I began to imagine how I can do it but at that time a thought came to my heart that if I die who will lose? I went and threw the scarf in the bin, and turned the television on and began to watch Oprah, I loved Oprah and I loved watching her shows that somehow she became my comfort. If was sad or feeling down, just give me Oprah Winfrey then I will be okay.

Thank God I had television but did not have that wisdom to run to the Bible, because reading Bible is as same as talking to God, God is the word and Bible is the word of God, From the beginning there was a word, a word was with God and a word was God. John 1:1

If I had been talking to God, no doubt I would not have reached where I reached, I did not care about God I was just running after money, and I did not have what it takes to make it. May be I didn't have any qualification, but if I was close to God, He would have made things easy I remember back in Uganda we had a saying which says that God helps those who help them selves. Some how its true, I was like someone running after a bird, can you catch it? Unless someone also has wings I did not care about God, and thank Him because He is not a man who will say, I told you so. The time I started searching for God was, when I had already given birth to my son, and I did not have a home of my own, I was living with other women in a charity home.

Good counsel network founded by Clare McCullough in West London. God bless her a million times, She gave my son and I shelter, God is using her to save lives of many children. God says in mark 10:14, let the little children come to me and do not stop them. When I was there

One of the ladies asked me to go to church with her, I was expecting to hear the word of God, but it was only deliverance and other things which I did not understand, she took me to church because she noticed that I had anger but then who can deliver anger from someone? Every time I went to church it was lining up and some people would lay hands on us, Sunday morning, evening service was the same. There was no worship and no preaching, I was attending every meeting but I did not find God, so it became just a routine and a waste of time. I thought God says, seek His kingdom first and everything will follow (Matthew 6:33). Nothing changed, anger is the worst enemy it is worse than witches, my advise to someone, don't think to much of your past, and don't fix your eyes on people otherwise you will be disappointed.

A time came and I said enough, I wanted to know God, and I wanted my life to be different, remember you cannot make a difference until you are different.

My most prayer God was, terminate the evil spirit of anger from me, I allowed anger in me because I was thinking too much of what I went through.

I started attending church services and reading my Bible more, at that time, I had left West London, but Clare was still supporting us she said, she will not stop until we have settled. She fulfilled her promises She gave us money to apply for our Visa, our documents were still in the home office, I did not have a job and I was in one room with my son. Sometimes I would be depressed because of not having work to do, but was reading Bible like never before, I started dreaming songs a lot, Whenever I go to bed, I would wake up singing songs of worship. And in the morning the first thing was to record to record them, was dreaming of songs a lot every time I closed my eyes, I would start singing or even seeing pictures the Bible. The beauty of it was whenever I was feeling sad, that is when I would start singing praises to God, which I have never understood why, in seated of complaining, a song would just come out. I started keeping my recorder near me because I knew I must get a song, on the train, in the supermarkets and every where. Its true God can change your misery into a ministry and He can turn your mourning into dancing. Jesus glory be to your name for all that I went through. One day I looked at myself and I was amazed by God's love towards me, and a song came to my spirit, who Iam I that you love me like this. Your love for me Jesus, I cannot understand it, and I don't know what I did, Jesus that you love me like this. I will worship you, if nobody will worship you, I worship you.

If I did not go through tough time these songs that I have written wouldn't have come out, When I was in Uganda I used to sing but I did not know the difference. That time songs did not mean anything to me, it was just like cramming a story and knows it all in my head, I did not have time, or wisdom to listen to the lyrics and to think about the meaning of the song. You cannot talk about what you don't know, most people sing what they have been through, there is no song that has no meaning.

Miriam sang song in Exodus 15:20 – 21, she sang, sing to the Lord for He has triumphed gloriously the horse and its rider, He has thrown into the sea.

I was not there, but she was praising God for victory over the Egyptians I imagine how they felt looking at their enemies drowning. Who can battle with God? He is A MAN OF WAR.

I got to a point that when I see a problem what I think of is the a song that will come out of it. And sometimes I would sing victory before a battle, one day I was cooking and from nowhere I started singing, God has dealt with my enemies Iam singing a song of victory! I wondered why I sang that song, but there was a battle somewhere and I won the victory in the name of Jesus. In 2012 I was told that we were going to be evicted from the house we were, I didn't know what do I looked at my 3 years old son,

I did not have money to rent even one room because I was not allowed to work at that time, I cried and said where will I put him? Then a song came to my head, Jesus, you will never forsake me, Jesus you will never leave me you care about me Jesus you will never leave me. Iam standing on the promises of Jesus, yes Iam standing on the word of Jesus, the word of Jesus is my sold rock. Iam counting every good promise that He has promised me because I know He will never lie to m, even though the wind blows I will not be moved, Jesus will hide me.

My testimony will encourage some one know that God can never forget you, you are in the palm of His hands, when He looks at His hands, He sees you.

I was so proud when I knew what it means to be the apple of God's eye, who can touch His eyes?

If I tell you I don't have adversaries, it will be a lie, but I don't really care if they fight or not all I have to do is worship my God. They tried many times to stop me from worshipping, how some one lose her voice without cough or flue? No sickness at all! It happened to me, in 2013 I early January I woke up early in the morning to worship, then I saw the whole room moving in circle but I said, I will not stop thought there was no strength in me. I held on to my bed and worshipped when I finished I went back to sleep, as I closed my eyes I saw snakes, dogs and cats in my room I don't know what happened, but I found my self wearing high heel shoes and as I stepped on them all, heads began to cut off. That is how they were defeated. Another time I got up in the middle of the night and decided to sing praises only, when I finished praising, I read my Bible then I went back to sleep, I wanted to relax a bit more since it was Sunday. I didn't believe what I saw, a woman was running without clothes on, I was holding a shiny sword in my hands chasing her. The week after we programme in London, when a man of God went to the altar he said, someone here your enemies will run naked! Don't aske me if I know the woman!! You can take anything you from me, but do not touch my worship and do not try my praises.

When you worship God you His heart, when you touch His heart you make Him happy, I imagine the King of all kings being pleased with you, you can ask Him for anything. There was a King who was pleased with the young girl because she danced before him and the he swore to give her anything, he even swore to give her half of his kingdom Matthew 14: 6-7.

The reason he told the her to ask for anything it's because she made him happy, you to can praise God and make Him happy. Sometimes when I wake up to worship God and tell Him, I greet you Jesus, Jehovah I salute you in the morning, I say good morning King of kings, take your seat Jesus and let me worship you, It's I can picture Him saying, I'm pleased. And when I tell Him that, You are the beautiful flower that never fades, Rose of Sharon, I worship you, I bow down for you, I worship You are the Master Planner that never fails, Rose of Sharon, I worship you, I can imagine Him saying thank you, no wonder I am blessed, You can't feed God and remain the same He does not eat food, if you want to quench His thirsty, give Him your worship, He yearns for it, in John 4:7, He asked a woman of Samara to give Him a drink! If you have been thirsty before and no one gives you a drop of water, then you will know how God feels if we don't worship Him.

Someone asked me that why is that any time I want to sing, I come up with war songs!! I also don't know but what I know, this world is full of battle, and you cannot fight a battle without an enemy. We all have our enemies within us Like anger, pride and then, we human beings made in the likeness of God fighting for each other, but why do wefight? Most of time it's envy and jealous, when these two enters a person, hatred must follow, some people can't stand to see others happy, they bleed. You may think that every one you call a friend, is happy to see you happy! I don't blame you because you don't know that Your friend might be your great enemy, wake up, If God can reveal who you call a friend, you will jump. I'm sorry to say this but it's true, I speak what I have seen, if you notice your friend acting funny because your level has changed, shift from him or he. You don't need permission to so, I didn't say you should suspicious but at the same time don't ignore warnings because you never know my cousin sang a song that says foes are bad. Do you know they can plot against a new born baby! Because they have seen his star shinning and their job is to stop it? failure is their end and downfall is their portion, I have seen evil returning back to them that plans it and f you don't believe it ask Haman an enemy of Jews I suggest that you read the whole book of Ether. The time and energy that someone spends in his or her secret corner planning evil for another person, is the same as another one spends in the secret place of the Most High God psalm 91:1 The difference is one is light and anther is dark. Oprah is not really a pastor but if you listen to her teaching, you will stop planning evil for to each other she said, anything thing that you do to people good or bad no matter what it will come back straight to your face. God help us what we do with these wicked people? They plan evil behind your back, what they don't know is there is a God heaven everything and He is able to reveal their plans. There is worldly song that says every move you take, I will be watching you there is no hiding place here except in Jesus. Every time I think about wickedness,

I remember Pharaoh king of Egypt his only problem was, the children of Israel were fruitful and mightier than them. Haters hate it when someone becomes fruitful, if you read Exodus 1:15-21 you will see that the solution to stop them from multiplying was to kill innocent baby boys. Did he know that what he did will one day come back to him? My 6 year old son told me that, it was the hand of God that kept Moses' basket floating on top of the river! And if you put it in another way it was because of Moses that Hebrew sons were killed, I think pharaoh though by doing that he will come across Moses, Satan spotted a deliver and he wanted to terminate his destiny. Who sent Pharaoh's daughter to go and bath at that time!

I'm not that good at Bible but Moses and Jesus had something in common when Jesus was born, He had a great enemy Herod. What pharaoh did is what Herod did, destroying Innocent children because of Jesus, but when he was planning it God appeared to Joseph in a dream and to told him to take the child to Egypt Matthew 2:13.

So God can reveal your enemy to you through dreams and tells you what your enemy is planning. When I talk about dreams I get a bit scared, because sometimes I see things, and wonder. My son's father was gone for some time we last saw him when the child was eight months old, but when he started school he saw other children with their fathers and he asked me, where was his father? I answered him that his father went on a business trip and he will come back. So it was towards Christmas he came and said, Mummy, daddy will come and tie my shoelace! When he said that I looked at him and said yes. Then I told God that the child He gave, me is a worshipper, Please bring his father Again, I told God that I was going to give Him a birthday present and He will also bring my son's father.

That Christmas I went and bought many Christmas card, And I wrote on them, this Christmas, I invite you to receive a gift that money can never buy, receive Jesus as your Lord and Savour, ask Him to come into your heart and you will never be the same again. I gave cards to all my neighbours, I would get up early the morning and put them through their letter boxes, because I know winning souls to Jesus is His heart beat. On Christmas day I missed a phone call when I listened to my voice message It was Isaiah's father! God really heard me In August 2014, he called again and said, he was coming It was Sunday we talked and everything was alright, then went to bed. When I slept I saw a woman fighting me, She was standing between my son and his father shouting, raising her hands and telling me, your son can't have his father back again, no he will not because my son's father left me! I didn't know that I was dreaming because it looked so real but when I woke up I knew it was dream, I have too much to say but this book will not contain it all, who can be against me, if God is for me?

Betty Amiina

Heavenly Father as we praise and worship you be blessed.

Song Number 1

OH SWEET JESUS

Oh sweet, sweet Jesus, how can I ever forget? How you suffered for me on the hill of Calvary
A friend of sinners, you are full of love, how can I ever forget?
How you suffered for me on the hill of Calvary
Our Redeemer Jesus you died to set me free, how can I forget?
How you suffered for me on the hill of Calvary

Song Number 2

KING OF GLORY

King of Glory the prince of peace, my Redeemer, I worship you
Mighty in battle, the strong deliveries, my Redeemer, I worship you.
The Great warrior, always a winner, my Redeemer, I worship you
You my tower, shelter, my hiding place, my Redeemer –
I worship you
Consuming fire, loving and patient, my redeemer
I worship you

Song Number 3

ROSE OF SHARON

Rose of Sharon I worship you
Rock of Ages I praise you
Glorious King I honour you
For you are holy, holy Jesus
You are holy, you are holy, you are holy, holy Jesus you

Song Number 4

BEAUTIFUL FLOWER

You are the beautiful flower that never fades
Rose of Sharon, we worship you
You are the beautiful flower that never fades
Rose of Sharon, we worship you
We Worship you we worship you
We bow down for you, we worship you
You are the Master Planner that never fails
Rose of Sharon we worship you
You are the beautiful Creator, the only artist
Rose of Sharon, we worship you

Song Number 5

THE MOST HIGH GOD

The most high God I worship you
I bow on my knees and worship you.
I bow on my knees and worship you
God Almighty I worship you
You have done us great and mighty things
Oh Lord who is like you?

Song Number 6

WHO SAID I WILL NOT WORSHIP YOU?

Who said I will not worship you?
Who said I will not worship you?
He's a liar, he's a liar, he's a liar, and he's a liar,
I will worship you Jesus, I will bow on my knees
And worship you
I will bow on my knees and worship you
You are an amazing God, you are an amazing God
Jesus I will worship you

Song Number 7

ALPHA AND OMEGA

Alpha and Omega, we give you all the glory
Alpha and Omega, we give you all the honour
Alpha and Omega, we give you all the praises
Alpha and Omega, we thank you very much
You are full of wonders, you are full of surprises
We bless you holy name, we lift you higher.

Song Number 8

ANCIENT OF DAYS

Ancient of days Daddy, I honour you
Ancient of days Daddy, I honour you
Ancient of days Daddy, I honour you
Ancient of days Daddy, I adore you
Ancient of days Daddy, I adore you
Ancient of days Daddy, I adore you
You will forever be the same
You will forever be the same
You will never, never change, you will never, never change
You will never, never change, you will never, never change
You will never, never die, you will never, never die
You will never, never die, you will never, never dies
Ancient of days Daddy, I honour you
Ancient of days Daddy, I adore you

Song Number 9

ROCK OF AGES

Rock of ages, we worship you
Rock of ages, we worship you
We worship your holy name, we worship you
We worship your holy name, we worship you

We honour you, we adore you
We worship you
Our God, our God, we worship you
Our God, our God, we worship you

Song Number 10

RIVER OF ABUNDANCE

We have come to the River of Abundance
We have come to the River of Abundance
We have come to drink the water of life
The water of life
We have come to drink the water of life
The water of life
We have come to River of Abundance

Song Number 11

THE STONE HAD BEEN ROLLED AWAY

The stone had been rolled away; the stone had been rolled away
He's alive, He is alive, and Jesus has risen.
He's alive, He is alive, and Jesus has risen.
Bow on your knees and worship Him
Bow on your knees and worship Him
The tomb is empty oh Jesus is risen
The tomb is empty oh Jesus is risen

Song Number 12

HOW I LOVE YOU MY REDEEMER

How I love you my Redeemer
How I love you my Redeemer
I love to give you all the glory; I love to give you all the glory

How I love you my Redeemer
How I love you my Redeemer
I love to give you all the praises; I love to give you all the praises

How I love you my Redeemer
How I love you my Redeemer
I love to give you all the worships; I love to give you all the worships

Song Number 13

YOU ARE MY JESUS

You are my Jesus you are my Jesus
You are my Jesus I will worship you
You are my Jesus you are my Jesus
You are my Jesus I will worship you
Forever more, forever more, forever more, forever more
Forever more, forever more
You are my Jesus I will worship you
You are my Jesus I will worship you
Impossible doer, I will worship you
Sovereign of God, I will worship you
Your Highness I will worship you
You are my Jesus I will worship you
Magnificent God, I will worship you
OHOOO I will worship you
King of kings, I will worship you
You are my Jesus, I will worship you
You are my Jesus, I will worship you
I salute you Lord of Lords,
You are my Jesus, I will worship you
I give you honour ohoo
You are my Jesus I will worship you
Among other gods I will worship you
You are the only living God
Oh Jesus, I will worship you

Song Number 14

I STEP IN JESUS

I step in Jesus, I step in Jesus, and I step in Jesus
I am available to worship you,
Jesus I am available, Jesus I am available;
Jesus I am available, I am available, to worship you

Song Number 15

MY GOD YOU ARE SO BEAUTIFUL

Oh my God, you are so beautiful
Oh my God, you are so beautiful
Oh my God, you are so beautiful
I tell you, you are so beautiful
I tell you, you are so beautiful
Oh Jesus, you are so beautiful
Oh Jesus, you are so beautiful
What you say is so beautiful
What you do is so beautiful

Lion of Judah you are so beautiful
You are so real, you are so beautiful
You are so real, you are so beautiful

Elohim, you are so radiant
Adonai, you are so radiant,
Baba, you are so radiant
You are so beautiful, Jesus you are so beautiful
You are so beautiful, Jesus you are so beautiful

Song Number 16

EVER PRESENT GOD

Ever present God, Jehovah Shammah
Ever present God, Jehovah Shammah
Ever present God, your name is Immanuel
Ever present God, your name is Immanuel
Your name is Immanuel, your name is Immanuel
Your name is Immanuel, God is with us

You will never forsake us, you will never forsake us
You will never forsake us, you will never leave us like orphans
You will never leave us like orphans

Song Number 17

POWERFUL GOD

Beautiful God, powerful God
Jesus I magnify you, I magnify you
I magnify you, Baba I magnify you
King of kings, Lord of lords, Jesus I magnify you
King of kings, Lord of lords, Jesus I magnify you

Wherever I go, wherever I go, I magnify you
Wherever I go, wherever I go, I magnify you
Among other gods, among other gods Jesus, I magnify you
In front of Nebuchadnezzar, Jesus, I magnify you

Song Number 18

MY CREATOR

My creator, my saviour I love you Jesus, I love you
My creator, my Saviour I love you Jesus I love you
I love you Jesus, I love you
I love you Jesus, I love you
I love you Jesus, I love you

My love for you is forever more, my love for you is forever more
My love for you is forever more
I love you Jesus, I love you
I love you Jesus, I love you, my love for not a secret
I love you Jesus, I love you

I announce my love for you; I announce my love for you
I announce my love for you
I love you Jesus, I love you

Because of who you are, I love you; Because of who you are I love you
Because of who you are, I love you
I love you Jesus, I love you
I love you Jesus, I love you
I love you Jesus, I love you

Song Number 19

THE ONE WHO DIED FOR ME

I will sing all the praises for the one who died for me
I will sing all the praises for the one who died for me
I will give Him all the glory; He is worthy to be praised
I will sing all the praises for the one who die for me

Song Number 20

JESUS DIED FOR ME

Jesus died for me, Jesus died for me,
Jesus died for me; He died, to wash my sins away
My saviour died for me, my saviour died for me,
My saviour died for me, he died to set me free
Hallelujah my saviour died for me
He died to set me free
He died to set me free
Jesus died for me; he died to set me free

Song Number 21

YOU ARE HOLY AND MIGHTY

YOU are, you are Jesus you are, You are holy and Mighty.
All creation, bow and worship you
All creation, bow and worship you.
For who you are, for who you are Jesus
You are holy and mighty.

Some 22

HALLELUJAH TO THE KING OF KINGS

Hallelujah to the king of kings, hallelujah to Lamb of God
Hallelujah to the king of kings, hallelujah to Lamb of God
King of kings, lamb of God, We worship you
King of kings, lamb of God, We worship you
King of kings, lamb of God, We worship you
King of kings, lamb of God, We adore you
King of kings, lamb of God, We adore you
King of kings, lamb of God, We adore you

Song 23

YOU ARE THE LIVING GOD

You are the living God you are the living God Jesus
You are the living God that's why I worship you
Oh Baba you are the living God, that's why I worship you
That is why I worship you

You are the only God you are the only God Jesus
You are the only God, that's why I worship you
You are the only God that's why I worship you
That's why I worship you

Song 24

I PRAISE YOU JESUS

I praise you, I praise you, and I praise you Jesus
I praise you, I praise you, and I praise you Jesus
I thank you, I thank you, I thank you Jesus
I thank you, I thank you, I thank you Jesus
I love you, I love you, I love you Jesus
I love you, I love you, I love you Jesus

Song 25

I BLESS THE NAME OF THE LORD

I bless the name of the Lord; I give Him thanks and praise
His name is Jehovah, He is worthy of my praise
He is the one who died for me
He is the one who is full of love
His name is Jehovah, He is worthy of my praise

Song 26

THE ONE I LOVE

You are the one I love; you are the one I cherish
You are the one I talk about all the time Jesus
Almighty God is your name; you are the one I talk about all the time
Almighty God is your name; you are the one I talk about all the time
Jehovah Nissi my, fighter you are the one I talk about all the time
Jehovah shalom, my peace, you are the one I talk about all the time
Elushadai is your name, you have more than enough for me
AS long as I have you, I will always have more than enough

Song 27

HEAVENLY FATHER

Heavenly father, we say thank you, you have done amazing you have done excellent
We offer you, our thanks giving, we say thank you
Thank you Jesus, we say thank you
We will exalt you o Lord our God
We will exalt you o Lord our God
We will tell every nation about your power
We will tell every nation about your works Jesus
We will exalt you o Lord our God

Song 28

GREAT IS OUR GOD

Great is our God, Great is our God
Sing praises to Him, sing praises to Him
Give thanks to Him, give thanks to Him
Proclaim His majesty, proclaim His majesty
Declare His power, declare His power
Lift His name higher, and bless Him always

Song 29

WE APPRECIATE YOU

We appreciate you, we appreciate you Jesus
We appreciate you our Father
Take all glory, take all the honour
We cannot thank you enough
We cannot thank you enough Jesus
We appreciate everything you have done for us.
We appreciate you Jesus

Song 30

MY REDEEMER

My Redeemer, my Redeemer
I will give you all the glory
I will give you all the glory
Jesus, Jesus, Jesus, I will give you all the glory
What you do, no man can do, what you no man can do
When I call on you, you really answer me
When I call on you Jesus, you really answer me
I will give you all the glory

Song 31

HOLY IS JESUS

Holy, holy, holy, holy, holy is Jesus
Holy, holy, holy is our God Almighty
Him alone is Holy Him alone is Holy
Holy is our God Almighty
Higher, higher, higher, higher, higher is Jesus
Higher, higher, higher, higher is our God Almighty
Him alone is higher, Him alone is higher
Higher is our God Almighty

Worthy, worthy, worthy, worthy, worthy is Jesus
Worthy, worthy, worthy, worthy is our God Almighty
Him alone is worthy Him alone is worthy
Worthy is our God Almighty

Song 32

GLORIOUS KING

Glorious Ancient of days
We bow down and worship you
You reign in majesty; we bow down and worship you
You reign in majesty

Song 33

JEHOVAH SHAMMAH

Jehovah Shammah, I praise you
From the bottom of my heart I worship you
With all my heart I love you
With all my hands, I lift you higher
For you are worthy Jesus
For you are worthy to be praised

Song 34

HE IS AN AWESOME GOD

He is an awesome God, let us praise His name
He is beautiful, let us praise His name
He is wonderful, let us praise His name
He is mighty, let us praise His name
He is powerful, let us praise His name
He is I am the I am, let us praise His name
He is our healer, let us praise His name
He is our rock, let us praise His name
He is higher, let us praise His name
He is glorious, let us praise His name
He is our hiding place, let us praise His name

Song 35

NO MATTER WHAT COMES TO MY WAY

I will praise you I will praise you Jesus
No matter what comes to my way
I will praise you, no matter what comes to my way
No matter what I see, Jesus, I will praise you
No matter what I hear, Jesus, I will praise you
No matter what I feel, Jesus, I will praise you
I will praise you, no matter what comes to my way

Song 36

MY LORD AND MY SAVOIR

My lord and my saviour my Lord and my saviour
My Lord and my saviour, you are so precious
It is an honour, it is an honour
To be in your presence and worship you
It is an honour to praise your name Jesus
It is an honour to bow before you Jesus

Song 37

GOD OF EVERYTHING

God of everything, God of everything
God of everything, your name is Adonai
God of everything, your name is Adonai
I give you glory I give you honour
I give you praises your name is Adonai
You are not a liar, you are not a loser
You are not a late comer, your name is Adonai

Song 38

MY REDEEMER I WORSHIP YOU

My Redeemer, my Redeemer, my Redeemer,
I worship you, my Jesus, I worship you my Jesus
God Almighty, God Almighty, God Almighty
I worship you God Almighty, I worship you
I worship you, I worship you, I worship you my Jesus
Lily in the valley, I worship you
I am that I am I worship you
I worship you my Jesus
Impossible doer, I worship you
KIng of kings I worship you, I worship you my Jesus
Original God, I worship you
I worship you my Jesus

Song 39

WE WORSHIP YOU GOD ALMIGHTY

We worship you, we worship you
We worship our God Almighty
We worship our God Almighty
You are alone are, our God, we worship you our God Almighty
Great I am we worship you, we worship our God Almighty
Jehovah Rapha, we worship you
We worship our God's Almighty

Song 40

FAITHFUL GOD

Faithful God, Jesus faithful God
Faithful God, Jesus faithful God
How I adore you
Faithful God, Jesus faithful God

I honour you faithful God
I bow before you faithful God

You are loving and patient faithful God
You are great and mighty and you are so beautiful
You never forget your promises
You are faithful to your promises
That is why I call you faithful God
Almighty God, I worship you
Almighty God, I adore you
Almighty God, you are so great
I bow before you and worship you my God
You so true, you are so worthy
Father Lord, I say thank you
Thank you Jesus

Song 41

I JUST WANT TO BLESS YOUR HOLY NAME

I just want to bless your holy name
I just want to bless your holy name
Jesus, King of kings saviour, Redeemer, creator
I just want to bless your holy name

Invisible God, I mmortal God, consuming fire, full of glory
I just want to bless your holy name
Omnipotent God, omnipresent God, sovereign King
I just want to bless your holy name

Song 42

WE SING PRAISES TO YOU

We sing praises to you, we sing praises to you
We sing praises to you most high
You are Almighty, God, great I am you do mighty oh Lord
You do wonders, you do miracles Awesome is your name
You are holy and worthy there is none like you
You are precious, you are beautiful, you are magnificent

Song 43

PRECIOUS KING OF GLORY

We worship you, precious king of glory
We worship you, great I am
We worship you, precious king of glory
We worship you, great I am

Precious King of glory there is no king like you
Precious great I am, there is no God like you
That is why we bow and worship you
That is why we reverence you

That is why we salute you
Precious king of glory there is no king like you
Precious great I am, there is no God like you

Song 44

I HAVE NO OTHER GOD

I know one I have, I know one God I have
The only God I Know, His name is Jesus
He is dressed in majesty, He is dressed in majesty
I have no other God beside you Jesus
There is no other God beside you Jesus
I have no other helper beside you Jesus
I have no other helper beside you Jesus
My help comes from you alone
There is no other helper beside you Jesus

Song 45

WE GLORIFY YOU

We glorify you, we glorify you
Our God, we glorify you, we glorify you
Our maker, we glorify you, we glorify you
Our healer, we glorify you, we glorify you
Our hope, we glorify you, we glorify you
Jehovah Nissi, we glorify you, we glorify you
King of glory, we glorify you, we glorify you

Song 47

I PRAISE YOU KING OF KINGS

King of kings dressed in power I praise you
King of kings clothed in honour, I praise you
King of kings seated higher I praise you

SONG 48

WORTHY IS THE LAMB

Worthy is the lamb worthy is the lamb
Who takes away the sins of the world
Worthy is the lamb worthy is the lamb
Seated upon the throne, seated upon the throne
He came from heaven because of love
A friend of sinners, hater of sin
To die for me, to die for you
To reconcile us back to the father
Lamb of God, I worship you
Lamb of God, I worship you

On the cross, at Calvary
Lamb of God you went for me
You were beaten because of me
Lamb of God I worship you
Lamb of God I worship you
He is calling, He is calling
He never wants anyone to perish
His hands are always open
To receive a sinner that comes to Him
Lamb of God I worship you
Lamb of God I worship you

Song 49

SPLENDOUR IN GLORY

Majesty, oh majesty
Splendour in glory
Majesty oh majesty
Mighty in power

Heaven and earth adore you
Heaven and earth adore you

Majesty King of kings
Heaven and earth adore you

Song 50

YOU ARE SO GOOD IN MY LIFE

Jehovah, Jehovah, Jehovah
You are so good in my life, so good so good
I will praise you for your awesomeness
I will praise you for your greatness
You are so good in my life, so good, so good

SONG 51

I WILL REVERENCE YOU

I will worship you, Jesus, I will worship you
I will worship you, because of who you are
I will worship you, because of who you are

I will salute you King of Kings
I will salute you
I will salute you because of who you are
I will salute you because of who you are

I will bow for you, Jesus
I will bow for you
I will bow for you, because of who you are
I will bow for you, because of who you are

I will reverence you Jesus
I will reverence you
I will reverence you, because of who you are
I will reverence you, because of who you are

Song 52

YOU ARE THE LAMP

Jesus you are the lamp
Jesus you are the lamp
Shining more than all the stars in heaven
Shining more than all the stars in heaven

I want to behold your glory
I want to behold your glory
You are the lamp shining more than all stars in heaven
You are the lamp shining more than all stars in heaven

I want to behold your glory
I want to behold your glory
You are the lamp shining more than all stars in heaven
You are the lamp shining more than all stars in heaven

You are so, so radiant you are so, so radiant
Jesus no word can explain it
Jesus no word can explain it
You are the lamp shining more than all stars in heaven
You are the lamp shining more than all stars in heaven

Song 53

KING OF ALL KINGS

King of all kings I worship you
King of all kings I worship you
King of all kings I love you
Your name is wonderful
Your name is wonderful

Gracious King only you, you are seated higher above
Only you, you are seated higher above
Only you, you are seated higher above
Jesus who can compare with you
Jesus who can compare with you

Your throne is in heaven
Your throne is in heaven
You rule by power and mighty
Jesus there is no king like you
Jesus there is no King like you.

Song 54

BREAD OF HEAVEN

Bread of haven Bread of heaven, Bread of heaven
I am so hungry
Draw me closer to you, draw me closer to you
Draw me closer to you; I am hungry to worship you
I am hungry to worship you
Living water, living water, living water
Jesus I am so thirsty
Draw me closer to you; I am thirsty to worship you
I am thirsty to worship you
What can quench this thirsty that I have?
What can quench this thirsty that I have?
Only to be in your presence
Only to be in your presence

Song 55

HALLELUJAH

Hallelujah, Hallelujah, Halleluiah, Hallelujah
Holy, Holy is our God, holy, holy is our God
Give Him honour hallelujah, halleluiah, adoration, hallelujah
Hallelujah, holy, holy is our God
Holy, holy is our God
Bow and worship Him hallelujah, bow and worship him
Bow and worship Him hallelujah, holy, holy is our God
Holy, holy is our God

Song 56

I WANT TO HONOUR YOU

Majesty, majesty, majesty
Majesty King of kings, I want to honour you
Majesty king of kings, I want to honour you

I want to give you thanks and praise
I want to give you thanks and praise
Majesty, I want to honour you
Majesty, I want to honour you

I want to bow and worship you
I want to bow and worship you
Majesty, I want to honour you
Majesty, I want to honour you

Song 57

GREAT I AM

Great I am, I worship you, Great I am, and I worship you,
Great I am, I worship you, King of kings, and I worship you

I lift my hands to worship you
Great I am I lift my voice to worship you
I lift my voice to worship you
Jesus King of kings, I worship you

I clap my hands to worship you
I clap my hands to worship you
Great I am, I clap my hands to worship you
Jesus King of kings I worship you

I clap my hand to worship you
I clap my hands to worship you
Great I am, I clap my hands to worship you
Jesus King of kings I worship you

Song 58

HOSANNA IN THE HIGHEST

Holy, holy, hosanna in the highest
Holy, holy, hosanna in the highest
Holy, holy, hosanna in the highest

Lamb who was slain, seated upon the throne
Lamb who was slain, seated upon the throne
Lamb who was slain, seated upon the throne
Holy, holy, hosanna in the highest
Holy, holy, hosanna in the highest

You died Jesus and rose again
You are a winner Jesus
You died and rose again
You are a winner Jesus
Holy, holy, Hosanna in the highest
Holy, holy, Hosanna in the highest

Song 59

MORNING STAR

Lamp upon the throne I worship you
Lamp upon the throne I worship you
God Almighty adore you
God Almighty I adore you

Jesus you are the lamp
I bow and worship you
You are brighter than the morning star
Jesus I bow and worship you

You are the light of the world
Jesus I bow and worship you
You are the saviour of the world
Jesus I bow and worship you

You are the only way the truth and life
Jesus I bow and worship you

Song 60

SAVIOUR OF THE WORLD

Saviour of the world, saviour of the world
Redeemer every knee worship you
Redeemer every tongue must proclaim your goodness

Song 61

SOVEREIGN God

Sovereign God Jesus Sovereign God
Sovereign God I worship you
Sovereign God I worship you

You are the God Almighty
You are the God Almighty
You are the God Almighty
Sovereign King I worship you
Sovereign King I worship you

There is power in your name
There is power in your name
There is power in your name
Sovereign King I worship you
Sovereign King I worship you

Song 62

HOW GREAT ARE YOU

Mighty God, Oh ooh Mighty God
Mighty God, oh ooh Mighty God
Mighty God, Oh Mighty God

How great are you
how great are you

I cannot understand your greatness
I cannot understand your greatness
I cannot understand your greatness
Mighty God, how great are you
how great are you
oh, oh how great are you

I stand in wow of you mighty God
I stand in wow of you mighty God
I stand in wow of you mighty God
Mighty God, how great are you
How great are you
how great are you

I cry in worship oh mighty God
I cry in worship oh mighty God
I cry in worship oh mighty God
Mighty God, how great are you
How great are you
Oh how great are you

Song 62

LION OF JUDAH

Lion of Judah, lion of Judah
Lion of Judah we worship you

Only God, only God, only on we worship you
Only God, only God, only on we worship you

Jesus, Jesus, Adonai we worship you
Jesus, Jesus, and Adonai we worship you

Song 63

HE'S AMAZING

He's amazing, He's amazing, and He's amazing
He's amazing, he's an Awesome God

Without any doubt the God I serve
Is amazing, is an Awesome God

He's lovely, He's lovely, and He's lovely
He's lovely, he's an Awesome God
Without any doubt, the God is serve
Is amazing is an Awesome God

Song 64

OUR REDEEMER

Our Redeemer oh, our Redeemer oh
Our Redeemer, we worship you
Our Redeemer, we worship you
Our Redeemer, we worship you

Redeemer, who come to save the world,
Lamb of God who come to save the world
We worship you, we worship you
We worship your majesty
We worship your majesty
Most Glorious, Your highness
We bow before your cross
We bow before your cross
We bow to worship you

Song 65

GREETINGS

Jesus I salute you, in the morning
Jehovah I say good morning,
Mighty God, I salute you in the morning
Jehovah I say good morning,
Your highness I salute you in the morning
Jehovah I say good morning

Jehovah, Jehovah, Jehovah
Jehovah I say good morning
I thank you for beautiful night
I thank you for the gift of new day
I thank you for the blessings for the day
Jehovah I say good morning

I thank you father for who you are
I thank you for your protection
I thank you for the angels around us
Jehovah is good morning

This is the day you have made for me
Nothing shall be impossible in your name
Jehovah I say good morning

Song 66

I EXALT YOU

Mighty God I worship you
Mighty God I worship you
I am that I am, great I am, and I exalt your name
I am that I am, great I am, and I exalt your name

Jesus I have come here to praise you
For you are wonderful to be praised

Jesus I have come to honour you
For your wonderful to be praised
Jesus I come here to lift you higher
For you are wonderful to be praised

Song 67

WE PRAISE YOU EVERYDAY

I am that I am, we praise you everyday
I am that I am, we praise you everyday
That is your name forever, we praise you everyday
I am that I am we bless you every day
That is your name forever, we bless you everyday

Song 68

JEHOVAH BEAUTIFUL

Jehovah beautiful, Jehovah beautiful
Jehovah beautiful, I mention your name everyday
I mention your name everyday

Jehovah Elohim, Jehovah Elohim
Jehovah Elohim mu I mention your name every day
I mention your name everyday

I declare your glory among the nations
I declare your glory among nations
Jehovah beautiful, I mention your name everyday
Jehovah Elohim I mention your name everyday

Song 69

CONSUMING FIRE

Consuming fire we worship you
Consuming fire we worship you

Consuming fire we worship you
Sweet aroma, Rose of Sharon
Sweet aroma, Rose of Sharon
Lily of the valley
Your presence is so sweet
Your presence is so sweet

You are so loving and caring, merciful God
You are so loving and caring, merciful God
Your presence is so sweet
Your presence is so sweet

Song 70

CAPITAL G. BAABA

BABA oh, BABA oh
BABA oh, BABA oh
Jehovah Nissi we worship you
BABA Jehovah Nissi,, we worship you
Jehovah Nissi, we worship you

BABA Capital G. Capital G. BABA God we worship you
BABA Big God we worship you
Big God, we worship you

Song 71

WE PROCLAIM YOU'RE MAJESTY

We bow on our knees and worship you King of Kings
We bow on our knees and worship you King of Kings
Lord of Lords we worship you
Lord of Lords we worship you

With a grateful heart, we lift your name on high
With thanksgiving we proclaim your majesty
We declare your glory and power Jesus

We say Adonai, Adonai, Adonai, we worship you
Adonai, Adonai, Adonai we worship you
Mighty God, Adonai, Adonai, we worship you
Lamb seated on the throne Adonai, we worship you

Thank you Father, I worship you God Almighty
Thank you Father, I worship you God Almighty
I adore you, I praise you
you are worthy, you are holy
You are awesome, you are wonderful
You higher lifted up.

Song 72

JESUS WHO NEVER CHANGES

Jesus who never changes
Jesus who never changes
Blessed be your name forever
Oh blessed be your name forever
Blessed Jesus, let your name be glorified

I thank you God full of glory
I thank you God full of glory
I thank you God full of glory
I thank you God full of glory
Blessed be your name forever

Song 73

HOLD MY HAND

Hold my hand, Jesus my saviour
Hold my hand, Jesus my saviour
Show me the way, show me the way Jesus
Take me to the gates of heaven
Take me to the gates of heaven
Light of the world, shine before me

Light of the world, shine before me
I want to see my way; I want to see my way Jesus
Take me to the gate of heaven
Take me to the gate of heaven

Song 74

I HONOUR YOU KING OF KINGS

I want to Honour you king of kings
I want to honour you king of kings
I am so grateful to bow before you
I honour you Lord of lords
I honour you king of kings
I long to see your throne, I long to see your throne
King of kings I honour you

Song 75

MOST BEAUTIFUL

Most beautiful, most handsome, most radiant
Most precious, most glorious, most wanted
Rose of Sharon, I worship you

Sweet perfume, sweet aroma
Rose of Sharon, I worship you
Beautiful morning star, beautiful morning star
Rose of Sharon I worship you

Song 76

BECAUSE OF WHO YOU ARE

Because of who you are Jesus; I will bow and worship you
Because of who you are Jesus; I will bow and worship you
Because of who you are Jesus; I will bow and worship you
You are the God Almighty, creator of universe

You are crowned with glory and honour Jesus
You are crowned with glory and honour Jesus
You are armed with strength and power
I will bow and worship you
Oh sweet Jesus, oh sweet Jesus
Beautiful love sweet caring darling, I praise you
Most high King I praise you

Song 77

CONVENANT KEEPING GOD

I worship you covenant keeping God
I worship you covenant keeping God
Oh covenant keeping God, I worship you
Jehovah, covenant keeping God, I worship you
God of Abraham, I worship you
God of Isaac, I worship you
God of Jacob, I worship you

You will never, never change I worship you
You will never, never change, I worship you
You will never, never lie, I worship you

Song 78

AWESOME FATHER

Awesome Father Jesus, Awesome Father Jesus
You are the God Almighty
Loving Father Jesus, loving father Jesus
You are the God Almighty

Loving Father Jesus, loving father Jesus
You are the God Almighty

Consuming Fire Jesus, Consuming fire Jesus
You are the God Almighty

Song 79

YOUR POWER IS AT WORK

King of Glory, your name is Jesus
King of Glory, your name is Jesus
Lord of host mighty in battle
Strong deliverer my defender
Consuming fire hedge around me
Your power is at work
Your power is at work
I trust in your name, your mighty name
Your powerful name, your mighty name
Your power is at work

Song 80

IN THE BEAUTY OF YOUR HOLINESS

In The beauty of your holiness Jesus
In The beauty of your holiness Jesus
I will come, I will come, Jesus I will come
I will come to worship you

In the beauty of your holiness Jesus
In the beauty of your holiness Jesus
I will bow; I will bow Jesus I will bow
I will bow and worship you

In the beauty of your holiness Jesus
In the beauty of your holiness Jesus

I will sing, I will sing, Jesus I will sing
I will sing and worship you

In the beauty of your holiness Jesus
In the beauty of your holiness Jesus
I will dance, I will dance, Jesus I will dance
I will dance and worship you

Song 81

ANCIENT OF DAYS

Ancient of days beautiful Rose of Sharon, with grateful heart, I bow before you
I bow before your feet and praise your holy name
Precious holy God I worship you
Precious holy God your name is wonderful
Oh Jesus your name is beautiful

Song 82

YOU REIGN ON HIGH

You reign in power, you rein power, and you reign in power
Jesus who died and rose again, Jesus who died and rose again
You reign on high, you reign on high, and you reign on high
Jesus who died and rose again, Jesus who died and rose again

See the King of glory who once was dead he is alive
Forever more, he defeated Satan, He defeated Satan
He is alive forever more
The key is in hands the key is in hands
He is alive forever more, the crown of thorns turned out to
be the crown of glory. He is alive forever more

Song 83

HOW I ADORE YOU

Jesus, Jesus, how I worship you
Jesus, Jesus, how I adore you
Jesus, Jesus, how I love you
Lion of Judah Jesus how I love you lamb of God
You love me yes I know I owe you my praise
I will fall; I will fall, in your presence
I will fall Jesus in presence, to bless your name
Every day you shower me with new blessings
Your mercies, I receive everyday
Faithful God I will fall in your presence and bless your name

Song 84

NUMBER ONE

Number one I worship you, Number one I worship you
Number one I worship you
It's you Jesus I am talking about
It's you Jesus I am talking about

Number one I praise you, number one I praise you
Number one I praise you
It's you Jesus I am talking about
It's you Jesus I am talking about

Number one I love you, number one I love you
Number one I love you
It's you Jesus I am talking about
It's you Jesus I am talking about

Number one I dance for you; number one I dance for you
Number one I dance for you
It's you Jesus I am talking about
It's you Jesus I am talking about
Number one I thank you, number one I thank you
Number one I thank you
It's you Jesus I am talking about
It's you Jesus I am talking about

Song 85

I LOVE TO WORSHIP YOU

I love to worship you, I love to worship you
I love to worship you, I love to worship you
God Almighty, I love to worship you
I can't do without is I love to worship you
I can't help it I love to worship you
I must worship you, I love to worship you

Glory in the midst of fire, I love to worship you
Hedge of fire, I love to worship you
Consuming fire I love to worship you
I am that I am I love to worship you
I am so grateful I must worship you

You can be anything, I love to worship you
You are my everything I love to worship you
I will sing for your everyday, I love to worship you

Song 86

I HAVE COME TO WORSHIP YOU

I have come to worship you Majesty
I have come to worship you Majesty

Majesty I want to praise you
Majesty I want to praise you
I have come to pour my worship on to you
I have come to pour my worship on to you

Let it please you, Jesus
Let it please you, Jesus
I have come to worship you

Song 87

WE GIVE YOU THE HIGHEST PRAISE

We bow down and worship you most high God
Most high God we bow down and worship you
At your feet we humbly bow
We give you the highest praise
We shout louder your praises
We bless you oh Jesus
The highest praise belongs to you

Betty Amiina

Song 88

AWESOME IS YOUR NAME

Awesome is your name, Awesome is your name,
Jehovah we praise you
Jehovah we praise you

Song 89

I WILL BOW AND HONOUR YOU

Will bow, I will bow, I will bow and honour you
Jesus I will bow and honour you
Ancient of days, Rock of ages
Jesus I will bow and honour you

I will fall, I will fall, I will fall, I will fall, I will fall and honour
Jesus I will fall and Honour you
Ancient of day's rock of ages
Jesus I will fall down and worship you

Song 90

YOU ALONE ARE WORTHY

You alone are worthy of our praise
You alone are worthy of our praise
Let us praise you Jesus
Let us praise you Jesus
Let us praise you Jesus
Let us praise you Lord of lords
Radiant king of glory, you must be praised

Song 91

NO OTHER NAME

There is no other name I can call except the name of Jesus
There is no other name I can call except the name of Jesus
There is power in the name of Jesus
There is power in the name of Jesus
Mighty power in the name Jesus

When I call the name of Jesus, impossible become possible
When I call the name of Jesus, bondage becomes freedom
When I call the name of Jesus, sickness becomes healing
There is power in the name of Jesus, mighty power in the name of Jesus

Song 92

HIGHER

Higher, higher, higher Jesus, higher we worship you
Higher, higher, higher Jesus, higher we worship you
I cannot compare anyone with you
Seated in the class of your own, seated in the class of your own
You are seated in the class of your own, Higher Jesus we
worship you, and Higher Jesus we worship you
Jesus we thank you Jesus, I thank you not because of what
you have done, but because of who you are
Not because of what you have done, but because of who you are
Oh higher Jesus we worship you

Jesus everlasting king, powerful and mighty
Jesus everlasting king, powerful and mighty
We worship you and exalt your name
We worship you and exalt your name

Song 93

WAY MAKER

Baba oh Baba oh
Way maker Baba ah, our hear, Baba oh
Our deliverer Baba oh
Oh big God you are, big God you are

You Trouble satan, you trouble Satan
An enemy of Satan
Baba big God you are

You confuse Satan, you confuse Satan
Oh big God you are, nothing is hidden from you
You know everything and you see everything
Oh Big God you are, big God you are

Song 94

STRENGTH OF ISRAEL

Lion of Judah, Lion of Judah the strength of Israel
Lion of Judah, lion of Judah, you are big and mighty, you are big and mighty
Heaven and earth belong to you; heaven and earth belong to you big and mighty

Song 95

ALL I HAVE TO SAY

All I have to say is I love you Jesus
All I have to say is I adore you
Wonderful Jesus, wonderful Jesus all I have to say is love

Everlasting father full of grace and love
You died that I can live all I have to say is I love you
Your body was broken for me
Your body was broken for me

Your precious blood was poured out for me
The crown of thorns your wore for me
All I have to say is I loving you

Your beautiful hands were pierced
Long nails went through your feet
You suffered shame and humiliation
You were hanged on the tree and left there to die
No one could ever understand your love
Love that came to look for a sinner like me

So what can I give you to show my appreciation?
Nothing but to worship you
Jesus all I have to say is I love you.

Song 96

I MAGNIFY YOU

Beautiful God, powerful God, Jesus, I magnify you,
I magnify you Jesus I magnify you
King of kings and lord of Lord Jesus I magnify you
I magnify you Jesus I magnify you

Wherever I go wherever I go Jesus
I magnify you Jesus I magnify you
Among other gods, among the other gods, Jesus
I magnify you, Jesus I magnify you
In front of my enemies, in front of my enemies Jesus
Jesus I magnify you, Jesus I magnify.

You will show your power Jesus. You will show your power
I look in front of me and I don't see any one who can
Help me, except you Jesus, you will show your power

Song 97

YOU ARE THE LIVING GOD

You are the living God, you are the living God Jesus
That is why I worship you that are why I worship you.

You are only God, you are only one Jesus.
You are the only one that is why I worship you.
You are the only one that can go through the fire and you-
Are not consumed, because you are a consuming fire, that is why I worship you.
All other gods are fake, all other are of silver and gold
All other gods are of stones and woods
God of gods that why I worship you.

if there is a God that I want to worship its only you
Jesus, its only you_ if there a Goa that I will
Bow for you it's only you Jesus.

Song 98

WHO CAN BE LIKE YOU

In my life in my life who can be like you Jesus?
In my life in my, life who can be like you?
Who can be compared to you? In my life Jesus!
Who can be equal with you? In my life Jesus!

You are too glorious, in my life Jesus.
You are too awesome in my life Jesus.
You are magnificent, in my life Jesus
Who can be compared to you, in my life Jesus!

You are too amazing in my life Jesus, you are too amazing!
You are too excellent, in my life Jesus
Rose of Sharon lion of Judah Lilly of valley,
Who can be equal with you?
You are too big to lie; you are too big to lie
You are too big to fail you are too big to fail.

Song 99

OUR GOD IS SO GOOD

Our God is so good, our God is so good.
Come let us praise Him, come let us praise Him
Come let us thank Him, come let us thank Him
Our God is so good.

Talk about His goodness talk about His love and talk
About his saving hand our is so good,
Talk about His sweetness He is sweeter than honey,
He is sweeter than sugar, our God is so good.

Beautiful God, sweet Jesus, you are so loving
And you are so kind
Jehovah Shammah, I praise you, from the bottom of
My heart I worship you, with all my heart I love you
With all my hands I lift you higher,
For you are worthy, you are worthy to be praised.

Because you are Jesus
I praise you and I worship you
Jesus I love you, who can be like you my Jesus!
I say no one and I say no one.
Your name is Yahweh, your name is powerful.

Great commander, Jehovah mighty in battle.
Strong deliverer, Jehovah Nissi
You are dressed in power, all authority belongs to you.

Song 100

ALL I WANT IS TO PRAISE YOU

All I want is to praise You; all I want is to praise You.
Jesus, the God almighty, my Saviour, all I want
Is to praise You, my healer, all I want us to praise You.

Adonai all I want is to praise You.
To give you all the glory to give you all the honour,
To give you all the praises.
That is all I want to do Jesus
That is all I want to do
Oh, I want you like never before, I want You like never
Before, I'm in love with you Jesus I want You like never before
I cannot do without you I want You like never before
to worship you I want you like never before.
To be in your presence I want You like never before
to serve you, I want You
Like never before.

Song 101

EVERYDAY

Every day of my life every day of my life
I will say thank you Jesus.
When I look around me, I see the reason to be so grateful.

Jesus you are so good to me, I have a reason to be so grateful

I have many many reasons to be grateful
Jesus I cannot count all my blessings.
They are too much for me to talk about
What shall I ever give you?
Only to worship you.

I thank you Jesus, because I know, beside you
Jesus there is no other God
As long as I live I will worship you Jesus.
Glorious king, I will adore you.
Rock of ages, ancient of day.
I will worship you Jesus.
Your name is Amen, your name is Amen.
Amen I will bless you forever.

Song 102

BE BLESSED FOREVER

I love you my Redeemer I love you my Jesus.
Be blesses forever, be blessed forevermore.
I love you my hope, I love you my Jesus.
Be blessed forever, be blessed forever more.
I love you my Defender, I love you my Jesus.
Be blessed forever be blessed forever more.
That is why I love you Jesus.
I am serving a God that never fails.
That is why I love you Jesus.
I am serving a God never lies.
That is thy I love you Jesus.
I am serving a God that loses.

Song 103

YOU WILL SHOW YOUR POWER.

You will show your power, Jesus.
You will show your power Jesus.
I look in front of me, I look around.
I don't see anyone, who can help me, except you Jesus

I fix my eyes on you my help comes from you alone

You are mighty, your power is so mighty.
I can feel your power, moving in this place,
Our God you is a Man of war, a Burner over us
Be thou glorified.

Song 104

YOU DESERVE TO BE LIFTED HIGHER

Jesus you deserve to be lifted higher.
You deserve to be lifted higher.
My maker higher, Lily of the valley higher.
In your presence I come with a grateful heart.
A heart of thanks giving, I come with a grateful heart, a heart
full of praise, I come I come with a grateful heart.
I believe everything about you, Elushadai, Elohim, you are God, I choose to praise you
No matter what. I choose to praise you.
Because our God you are a great God! Your understanding
Is infinite.

Song 105

ALL THE TIME

I will worship you Jesus, I will worship you Jesus.
All the time I will worship you.
Nothing can stop me oh nothing can stop me.
In the middle no who where in middle nowhere
I will worship you.
In the middle of fire, in the middle of fire
I will worship you.
In front of Nebuchadnezzar, in front of Nebuchadnezzar
I will worship you
Are you not the only one who has the power, to deliver me?

Song 106

SOMETHING PRECIOUS

Something more precious than silver and gold
Is the name of Jesus, oh how I love the name of Jesus
How I love the name of Jesus.
There is power mighty in the name of Jesus

There is healing in the name of Jesus,

There is freedom in the name of Jesus,

How I worship your name Jesus,
How I worship your name Jesus.
How I praise your name Jesus,
How I praise your name Jesus,
How I praise your name Jesus
Stronger and majesty, strong and mighty
You a wonder working God.

Song 107

WHAT SHALL I A RENDER?

What shall I a render to you? As I am what
Shall I render?
Before you Jesus I come as I am what shall I a render
You daily load me with benefits
You supply my needs everyday
You fill my cup, it over follows,
What shall I a render?
I will come before you with a beautiful song in my mouth.
with a grateful heart I will bow and worship you.
Oh what shall I arender.

Song 108

WONDERFUL JESUS

Oh yes, Oh wonderful Jesus,
I will never be hungry, I will never luck anything
My father is Jehovah Jireh
Oh wonderful Jesus.

I will never be sick, I will never be sick,
My father is Jehovah Rapha

I will never lose a battle, victory is mine because
My father is Jehovah Nissi the Man of war.
Oh wonderful Jesus.
I will never be alone, I will never be forsaken.
My father is Jehovah shammah ever present.
God,
And I will always have everything I need. I will
Never be a beggar, my father is Elushadai, more than enough.
God of abundance, all sufficient God.
Oh wonderful Jesus

Song 109

I FEEL LIKE WORSHIPPING YOU

I feel like worshipping you Jesus.
I fell like worshipping you; Jesus your presence is so sweet
I feel like talking to you Jesus, Jesus I feel like
talking to you, your voice is so sweet.
You show me the pass of life, in your
Presence there is fullness of joy and at your right hand pleasures forever more.

It's only you Jesus, who else can do?
Its only you who has power, it's only you
who has a final word, who
Else can do?
It's only you who has a garment of healing Jesus
That is why I want to be in your presence everyday
There is life in your presence.

Song 110

GREAT AND MAJESTY

Your highness Jesus great and majesty
I salute you great and majesty.
Great is your power wonderful is your name
God the father, God the son, Holy Spirit I adore you.

Powerfully and Mighty, holy and Awesome
you are the God who saves, let us bow and worship you, Saviour of the world
Redeemer, Every knee must bow and worship you,
Ever tongue must declare your power.

Song 111

JESUS INCREASE IN ME

Increase in me Jesus increase in me.
Oh yes Jesus increase in me.
Have your way in me Jesus, have your way in me.
Jesus, Increase in me.
Empower me Jesus, empower me, oh yes
Jesus increase in me.
Be my teacher Jesus, be my teacher every day.
Jesus increase in me.
Be my controller Jesus be my controller
Yes Jesus increase in me,
Show my your ways Jesus, show me your ways
I pray oh yes Jesus increase in me.
Use me as you want Jesus, use me,
Oh yes Jesus increase in me.

Song 112

YOU RULE IN POWER

You rule in power, you rule in majesty
With a rode of Ion in your hands your name is Elusdai

When you speak the world trembles.
Consuming fire and loving father your name is Elshadai

Who will not fear you Jesus you burn in water
Fire goes before you, your name is Elushadai

Your love never comes to an end Jesus.
You have new mercies every morning, your name is Elushadai.

Song 113

WHEN I LOOK AROUND

When I look around I see your hand and I say thank you
I stand in wow of you Jesus.
When I see the work of your hand, how you formed the world
When See the clouds, sun, stars and the moon

Jesus I stand in wow of you.
Thank you or everything you made them so beautiful
Thank you for the sunshine, thank you for the rain.
Thank you for snow, thank you for cold summer and winter.
Your wisdom is beyond my understanding.
Thank you our creator.

Song 114

WHAT A WONDERFUL GOD

What a wonderful father, what a wonderful God, we praise you, we thank you,
My heavenly father I woke up with new song
In my heart
To praise you, to honour you, to bless you, I woke up with a new song in my mouth
Not because of what you have done, but because of who you are.
YOU REIGN ON HIGH JESUS
You reigned on high Jesus, you are higher than heavens.
Glorious king the only one who will reign forever

I just want to bow down before your throne.
As the angels worship you Jesus, as the angels worship you, I want to be included.

Heaven and earth shall pass away but you King of Kings shall reign forevermore
I lay myself at your feet, Jesus because
I was born to worship you
I want to number one to worship you let me
Pour my praises on to you.

Song 115

I KNOW WHO YOU ARE

I know who you are oh my Jesus.
I know who you are Aba father.
I know who you are oh my Jesus, I know who you are oh.
You are the mighty, mighty healer.
You are the mighty deliverer.
Strong in battle, you have never lost any battle.

Oh my Jesus I know who you are
I know who you are Abandoned father.
You are the one who makes lame the walk.
You are the one who makes the blind see.
You are the one I love Jesus.

You are the one makes mute to speak, You are the one brings the dead back to life.
You are the one sets the prisoners free.
You are the one I love Jesus.

You are the one says yes, nobody can say no.
You are the one say no, nobody can yes.
You are the one opens the door and nobody can shut it.
You are the one shuts the door and nobody can open it.

Song 116

SING FOR JESUS

Dance for Jesus, dance for Jesus...
With all your mind, with all your mind
Dance for Jesus.

Sing for Jesus, sings for Jesus
With all your strength, with all your strength.
Sing for Jesus.

Clap for Jesus, clap for Jesus.
With all your power with all your power.
Clap for Jesus.

Sing for Jesus, sing for Jesus
With all your heart, with all your heart.
Sing for Jesus.

Walk for Jesus, walk of Jesus.
With all your strength, with all your strength,

Jump for Jesus, jump for Jesus
With all you have, with all you have.
Jump for Jesus.

Song 117

YOU ARE MY EVERYTHING.

Jesus, you are my everything, Jesus you are my everything
I will depend on you, Jesus I will depend on you
Because I know, you are my everything.

I will believe I you, Jesus I will believe in you
Because you are my everything.

I will wait on you, Jesus I wait on you.
Because I know, you are my everything.

I will trust in you, Jesus I will trust in you.
Because I know, you are my everything.

I will rely on you, Jesus I will rely on you.
Because I know you my everything.

I will lean on you, Jesus I will lean on you.
Because I know, You are my everything.

I will hide in you, Jesus I will hide in you.
Because in know you are my everything.

I will hope in you, jess, I will hope in you
Because I know, you are my everything.

Song 118

A FRIEND OF SINNER

Jesus a friend of sinners, Jesus a friend of sinners
He was nailed on the cross
Jesus our saviour, Jesus our Savour
He was nailed on the cross, Jesus a friend of sinners

Because of His love he died to save us
Jesus a friend of sinners

Nothing can wash our sins except the blood of Jesus
Which He shade at Calvary
Jesus a friend of sinners

Dip yourself in His blood, dip yourself in His blood
Jesus a friend of sinners

Say no to Satan, receive the love of Jesus
Receive the love of Jesus
Jesus a friend of sinner

See how He is calling, come to me you sinners
Come to me I love you, Jesus a friend of sinners
See how He was beaten, the crown of thorns
On His head, He crucified with robbers,
Jesus a friend of sinners

Song 119

HIGHEST

Highest, highest we praise you
Highest, highest we dance for you
I will dance for you, because you are wonderful
I will sing for you, because you are beautiful
Jehovah you are wonderful
Jehovah you are beautiful

Song 120

GLORIOUS KING

Glorious king, you are so radiant
You are brighter than a sunny day, you are brighter than a shining star
You are so beautiful to be hold Jesus
You light my way, I see everything in a new light
You are more beautiful than a crystal glass
You are more beautiful than the precious stone

YOU ARE THE ONLY ONE

You are the only one Jesus worthy of my praise
I will never praise another god, Jesus you are the only one worthy of my praise

How can I worship another God, Jesus you are the only one worthy of my praise
I will bow for you alone; you are the only one worthy of my praises
Why should I search for another god? You are the only one worth of my praise

Song 121

ALMIGHTY KING OF KINGS

Almighty God, Almighty king of kings
Your throne is forever more
You rule in heave and earth
Your throne is forevermore
You make kings, you remove kings; I removable

Your throne is forever more
I have a father His name is Jesus Mighty in battle, Jehovah nissi.
In times of trouble, He is my defender
He will never leave me, He will never forsake me
He is ever present God, He is always with me
Jesus how can I not I love you
Your love for me is unspeakable
Your love for me is immeasurable
Where can I go from your presence?
I have no other God who is like you
Ready to catch me in case I fall down
Your love for me took you Calvary to die for me
Almighty God you died a shameful death
You were mocked, spat on, you wore a crown of thorns
Forever Jesus I will worship you, where you picked me, nobody knows except me
Let me stay in your presence giving you glory
You gave me a touch that made me whole

Song 122

AMONG THE NATIONS

Among the nations I will praise you, among the people will worship you
Be exalted our God above heavens
Be magnified you offspring of David son and God, servant and Kings
Maker of all universe, humble and highly exalted, I will
praise you Lord, from the bottom of my heart
I worship you with all my heart
I love you with all my heart
I lift you higher for you are worthy
Jesus worthy to be praised.

Song 123

HOLY GOD

Holy God most high king, I fall on my knees before you
I fall on my knees before your throne

I bow before you most precious, Glorious King, I humbly worship you
Jesus who died my only hiding place
You are my solid rock where I stand
And my running place, you hold me in palm of your hands under your shadow
You keep me no one can take my praises, all the praises belong to you Jesus

Song 124

I AM SO GRATEFUL

I am so happy, I am so grateful Jesus
For everything you have done for me
I am so grateful
For the breath, I breathe every day, for sleep every night
And in the morning you wake me up
Jesus I am so grateful

For your hands that hold me every day, you are the pillar that holds my life
Jesus without you I cannot do anything, you are my potter, you keep safe in your care
Jesus you bless me every day, you are so kind to me, and I cannot count all my blessing
Your mercies are new every morning My God you are so good to me
You are not a liar, you are not a liar
I believe in you
You are not a loser, I trust in you
And you are not a late comer Jesus
You are always on time
Oh Jesus that is how good you are
who is like you?
Who can love me more than you love me?
Who can hug me like you? Who can feed me like you?
My navigator, the driver of my life
Who can be compared to you?
Who can take care of me like you?
Who can direct me like you?
Number one Jesus, I praise you and bless your name

Song 125

I LOVE YOU SO MUCH

I love you so much, you are my God
My everything Jesus, I love you so much
My healer, my provider, my only one
I love you so much

Jesus I want to tell you that I love you from the bottom of my heart
I can not explain how much I love you
There is no word to explain it.
No interpreter can give me the meaning
Jesus I love you
I love you because you first loved me, my beautiful saviour
My deliverer, my hope, my lifter
You are a winner, my battle fighter, Jesus
Victory is mine
I love you, Oh I love you so much

Only God and king, you rule in heaven and earth
You defeated Satan, you defeated an enemy
You accomplished your mission
Oh I love you so much
I cherish you Jesus, Big and powerful
Great and mighty, I cannot measure you love for me

Song 126

I KNOW WHY

I know I know that you are God, Jesus, I know why
I know that you are God
You created all things, that is why I know that you are God
Before the world was made you were already in existence
At your word Jesus all things were created
That is why I know that you are God

You created me in your likeness Jesus
You breathed into my life, the breath of life
And you gave me life when you died at Calvary
That's why I know that you are God
You destroyed the work of Satan,
Jesus that is why I know that you are God
I was a sinner, number one sinner Jesus
I was in darkness, you brought light to me
You gave me peace of mind, you gave me victory
Halleluiah, that is why I know that you are God

I can not stop thinking about what you have done for me
I have a reason to call you God because you have done excellent in my life
I have seen wonders and miracles that's why I know that you are God

Song 127

YOU REIGN ON HIGH

You reign on high Jesus, you are higher than heavens
Glorious King, the only one who will reign forever
I just want to bow down before your throne
Heaven and earth shall pass away, but you king of kings, shall live forever more
I lay my seat at your feet because; I was born to worship you
As the angels worship you Jesus I want to be included
I want to be number one to worship you
So let me pour my praises on to you

Be lifted up King Jesus, be lifted up you are the king of kings, see
the king of glory who once was dead is alive forever more
He defeated Satan, He's alive forevermore
The crown of thorns has turned to be the crown of glory
He's alive forever more

Song 128

LET HEAVEN WORSHIP HIM

Our God reigns let the earth worship Him
Our God reigns let heaven worship Him
Let us worship our God who reigns and lives forever
Let us praise and exalt His name

We lift our hands with thanksgiving
Our father we worship you
We want you like never before, we long to glorify you
Our desire is to bless you everyday
We long to be in your presence
Jesus you are more than enough and you have done enough what no one can do.
We can not explain the love you have for us, but we can experience it
Carpenter Jesus, humble King you are highly exalted

Song 129

I HAVE A SONG FOR YOU

My Redeemer who went on the cross for me
I have a song for you; I have a song to sing for you
As birds in the trees have their own melody, and have their reasons to sing
I also have a reason to sing for you
You paid the highest price in full you bought me with your precious blood
Who else could have done it for me?
I will sing with my eyes fixed in heaven
For you searched, until you found me
Jesus, I was bound, you broke chains, I am now free
you brought me from slavery
For that reason my lips will sing for you
You lived a good life, and you died a criminal death
Shamefully you were hanged on a tree
For this reason my mouth will praise you

Song 130

HEAVENLY CHOIR

I join heavenly choir Jesus
I join heavenly choir Jesus
As the angels sing hallelujah
I bow, I bow, bow Jesus
I bow on my knees and worship you

Great I am, I worship you
Great I am, I adore your name
I declare your power Great I am
I proclaim your Majesty
Great I am I worship you

Oh God you are never too much in my life
I can't get enough of you
I want to worship you always
To sing holy, holy, glory to you Jesus

Oh Yahweh, Yahweh, Yahweh
You are worthy, you are worthy of my praises
Yahweh you are worthy of my worship

Song 131

WONDERFUL SAVIOUR

Sweet Jesus wonderful saviour, so loving and so kind
Redeemer, we worship you
We bless your holy name, heavenly father be the exalted
Darling Jesus, so sweet, so precious
We praise your holy name

Song 132

I WANT TO WORSHIP YOU

I want to worship you, I love to worship you
I love to worship you
God Almighty I love to worship you
I can't do without it I love to worship you
I can't help it I love to worship you
Hedge of fire around me I want to worship you
Consuming fire I love to worship you
Glory in the midst of fire, I love to worship you
You can be anything, I love to worship you
You can do anything, I want to worship you

Song 133

I WILL FALL

Oh Jesus you are Awesome
Jesus you are Awesome
I will fall and worship you
I will fall and worship you
At your feet I will fall
At your feet I will fall
Angels bow before you
Angels bow before you
They sing holy, holy is the lamb
They sing holy, holy is the lamb
I joined heavenly angels
I joined heavenly angels
To sing holy, holy to the lamb
To sing holy, holy to the lamb

Be lifted higher Jesus
There is no other God except you
There is no other God except you
You walk with me in the fire

71

You walk with me in the fire
There is no other God except you
In the sea Jesus you are with me
In the ocean you are with me
You promised never to leave me
There is no other God except you
Be lifted higher, higher there is no other
God except you

Song 134

NOBODY

Jesus you are so good
Elushadai you are so good
No-no-no-no, I don't know any one Jesus
No-no-no-no, noone is like you
No-no-no-no, no one like you

Noone can be compared to you Jesus
No one can be compared to you
You are seated in the class of your own
can be equal to you
Oh Jesus you are so good
In the morning I woke up and say good morning sir
With my hand lifted up to you, I greet you
I praise you, for you keep me safe in your hands
You watch over me thank you

Song 135

BECAUSE

Thank you for being almighty warrior
Thank you for being almighty warrior
Because I carry you Jesus
Because I carry you Jesus
Enemies free before you

Enemies free before you
Enemies free before you

Because I carry you fire
Because I carry you fire, demons tremble before
Thank you Jesus, for being a mighty warrior
Thank you Jesus, thank you

Song 136

I WORSHIP A GOD

I worship a God that is so mighty
I worship a God that is so powerful
Nothing is impossible for Him to do
Oh I worship a God that is so mighty
I worship a God that is so powerful
My God can shake a mountain
My God can walk on water
I know my fighter can never lose a battle
I know my fighter can never lose a battle
Jesus, Jehovah Nissi
His eyes are flames of fire
He is a consuming fire
That is why I love Him
That is why I worship Him
A sharp sword, comes out of His mouth
And He burns in water
That is why I love Him
That is why I worship Him

Song 137

I PRAISE JESUS

I praise Jesus with all my heart
Oh I praise Jesus with all my heart
I praise Jesus will all my soul

I praise Jesus will all my soul
I praise Jesus, I praise Jesus
I praise Jesus will all my soul

I praise Jesus with all my hands
I praise Jesus with all my hands
I know, I praise Jesus, I praise Jesus
I praise Jesus with all my soul

I praise Jesus with all my fingers
I praise Jesus with all my fingers
I know, I praise Jesus, I praise Jesus
I praise Jesus with all my fingers

I praise Jesus with all my legs
I praise Jesus with all my legs
I know, I praise Jesus, I praise Jesus
I praise Jesus with all my legs

I praise Jesus with all my shoulders
I praise Jesus with all my shoulders
I know, I praise Jesus, I praise Jesus
I praise Jesus with all my shoulders

I praise Jesus with all my feet
I praise Jesus with all my feet
I know, I praise Jesus, I praise Jesus
I praise Jesus with all my feet

I praise Jesus with all my toes
I praise Jesus with all my toes
I know, I praise Jesus, I praise Jesus
I praise Jesus with all my toes

I praise Jesus with all my back
I praise Jesus with all my back
I know, I praise Jesus, I praise Jesus
I praise Jesus with all my back

Song 138

JEHOVAH WE WORSHIP YOU

Jehovah, oh Jehovah, Jehovah we worship you
Jehovah we worship you

How great is your name Jehovah!
Jehovah we worship you
How Awesome is your name Jehovah!
Jehovah we worship you

How glorious is your name Jehovah!
Jehovah we worship you
How precious is your name Jehovah!
Jehovah we worship you

How beautiful is your name Jehovah!
Jehovah we worship you
How amazing is your name Jehovah!
Jehovah we worship you

Jehovah, oh Jehovah
Jehovah we worship you

Song 139

BEAUTIFUL MORNING STAR

Beautiful morning Jesus, beautiful morning star
Beautiful morning, you are so shining
Sweet perfume, Sweet perfume, Sweet perfume
You are so shining

Beautiful morning star, I praise you right now
Beautiful morning star, I praise you right now
Beautiful morning star Jesus you are so shining

Betty Amiina

Beautiful morning star, I thank you right now
Beautiful morning star, I thank you right now
Beautiful morning star Jesus you are so shining

You light my way everyday
You light my way everyday
Beautiful morning star Jesus you are so shining

Song 140

ALPHA AND OMEGA

Darling Jesus it's an honor to worship you
You are the king of kings Alpha and Omega
Who was dead and alive forever more
You are the king of kings alpha and omega
Who was dead and now alive forever more

Jesus I have come here to worship you
To fall down at your feet
To tell you how beautiful you are
Sweet Jesus you are so wonderful

Oh darling Jesus, darling Jesus so precious and so sweet
We worship you, we praise your holy name
Sweet Jesus wonderful saviour
So loving and so kind, we worship you
We bless your great name heavenly father
Be thou exalted

Song 141

FROM THE RISING OF THE SUN

From the rising of the sun
From the rising of the sun
To it's going down, Jesus I will worship you

who will worship our God?
Who will worship our God?
Come on, join, and come on join me
To worship our God
Who will worship Him? Who will worship Him?

Jesus is yearning for our worship
Jesus is yearning for our worship
He is sitting at the well, He is waiting
For who will worship Him

Jesus is thirsty for our worship
He is waiting for who will give Him a drink
Give Jesus a drink; He is waiting for who will worship Him
Come on join me come on join me
To worship our God

Song 142

I HUMBLY WORSHIP YOU

I humbly worship you Jesus, I humbly worship you
My heart magnifies you
My heart magnifies you
I bow in humble adoration, I bow in humble adoration
Father can you see how much I adore you?
Can you see father, Can you see father?
Can you see how much I adore you?
Father look at me, Father Look at me
Can you see how much I adore you?

Song 143

HOSANNA

Jesus who died for me, my hiding place
My solid rock where I stand, I give you glory and honour
Hosanna Hosanna

Hosanna in the highest, Hosanna in the highest
We praise you hosanna we bless you hosanna
We honour you hosanna, Hosanna in the highest

Glory be to your name, Glory be to your name
Glory be to your name, Hosanna in the highest
You are higher than heaven, you are higher than heaven
Hosanna in the highest

We bow down and worship, we bow down and worship
We bow down and worship, hosanna in the highest
We lift our voice to worship
We lift our hands to worship
We cry in worship
We cry in worship
We cry in worship, hosanna in the highest

Song 144

POUR YOUR RAIN ON US

I sing Hallelujah, I sing Hallelujah
Pour your rain on us
Pour your rain on us
So we can be wet
I sing Halleluiah, I sing Halleluiah for your rain on us

Jesus you're the strong tower, you are the strong tower
You are bigger than anything we can imagine
You are bigger than anything we can imagine
So pour your rain on us
We want to be wet

Song 145

I CRY INN WORSHIP

You are holy, you are holy
You are holy Awesome Jesus
You are holy Awesome Jesus

God Almighty Alpha and Omega
Beginning and end, I worship you
You are the only King who will reign forever
You are holy Awesome Jesus

I bow in worship, I bow in worship
I bow in worship
I join heavenly choir to worship you
You are holy awesome Jesus

You are beautiful, you are mighty
You are so glorious king of kings
I cry in worship, I cry in worship
I sing Hosanna to the Lamb of God

Oh Jesus you are awesome
I will fall and worship you
I will fall down at your feet
I will fall down at your feet
I will fall and worship you
Angels bow before you
Angels bow before you

Song 146

LIGHT THE WORLD

Jesus I have come to worship you
To fall down at your feet
To tell you how beautiful you are, sweet Jesus

You are so wonderful
You are beautiful Jesus, lily of the valley
You are so beautiful
You are brighter than the morning star
Light of the world, we worship you

Song 147

JEHOVAH WE PRAISE YOUR NAME

Jehovah, Jehovah, Jehovah we praise your name
Jehovah we praise your name

Your name be blessed forever more
Your name be blessed forever more
Jehovah we praise your name
Your name is a tower, your name is rock
Your name is sword, your name
There is no other name I can call only the name of Jesus.

There is no other name higher than the name of Jesus
There is no other name, there is none
Your name is wonderful, your name is powerful
Your name is mighty to save
Your name is mighty to heal; your name is my weapon
Your name is fire
Jehovah we praise your name
At the sound of your name, enemy must leave
At the sound of your name the enemy must bow
Nothing resists the of Jesus Jesus

Song 148

MAJESTY SEATED HIGHER

Majesty seated higher above
Majesty seated higher above
All creation bow and worship you

All creation bow and worship you
You are the king who will reign forever

I will bend and praise you Jesus
I will bend and praise you
With all my hands, lifted up, I will bend and praise your name
For you are good, for you are good
For you are good, for you are good
For you is good,
Alpha and Omega

Song 149

I'M HERE TO WORSHIP.

I am here to worship you
I am here to worship you
I am here to wash your feet
I am here to pour my praise on you
I am here to anoint your feet
I am here to bless you Lord
Jesus as I worship you, let me feel the wonder of your touch.

Song 150

INN THE BEAUTY

In the beauty of your holiness
In the beauty of your holiness
In the beauty of your holiness
I will sing and praise you Lord

In the beauty of your holiness
In the beauty of your holiness
In the beauty of your holiness
I will bow and worship you
Because you are a caring Father
Because you are a caring Father
Great God, Great God
I will worship you forever more

Song 151

REMAIN IN YOUR PRESENCE

I have come to bow down for King of Kings
I have come to bow down for you, Jesus
Let me remain in your presence
Let me remain in your presence
Where you are, I want to be
Where you go, I want to go
Jesus I want to hear your voice everyday
Let me remain in your presence
I want to be a tree planted in your house
I want to be a tree planted in your house
Jesus let me remain in your presence

I want to be a worker in your garden
I want to be a worker in your garden
Jesus let me remain in your presence
I want to clean your house everyday
I want to clean your house everyday
Let me remain in your presence
I want to sing for you every day
I want to feel your touch everyday
Let me remain in your presence
Peace and hope are found in your presence
Strength and joy are found in your presence
Jesus where can I go from you
There is no other God I know, who can hold me like you

Song 152

I GIVE YOU PRAISE

I give you praise, I give you praise
I give you praise Mighty God

Mighty to save, Mighty to save
Mighty to save, mighty to praise
Mighty to deliver, Mighty to deliver
Mighty to deliver, I give you praise

Mighty to heal, mighty to heal
Mighty to heal, I give you praise
Mighty to answer, mighty to answer
Mighty to answer, I give you praise

Mighty to fight, mighty to fight
Mighty to fight, I give you praise
Mighty in battle mighty in battle
Mighty in battle, I give you praise

Song 153

SONG OF THANKSGIVING

With songs of praise I come to you Jesus
With songs of praise I come to you
With songs of praise I come to you Jesus
My heart is grateful
My heart is grateful

Songs of thanksgiving I will offer you Jesus
Song of thanksgiving I will offer you
Song of thanksgiving I will offer you
My heart is grateful
My heart is grateful

I will enter your presence Jesus; I will enter your presence
I will enter your presence with thanks giving and praise
I will enter your presence with thanks giving and praise
Because I appreciate you
Because I appreciate you, King of kings
I will bow on my knees; I will bow before you Jesus
I will bow and worship you

Song 154

YOUR THRONE

Before your throne, before your throne
Before your throne, before your throne
Before your throne I will bow
I will bow, I will bow
I will bow before you King of kings
I will bow and worship you

Before your throne I will dance
I will dance; I will dance before you King of Kings
I will dance and worship you

Before your throne I will sing
I will sing, I will sing, I will sing before you king of kings
I will sing, I will sing
I will sing and worship you

Before your throne I will jump
I will jump before you king of kings
I will jump, I will jump, and I will jump and worship you

Before your throne I will crawl
I will crawl before you king of kings
I will crawl, I will crawl, and I will crawl and worship you

Song 155

SING WITH ME

Will you sing with me this song?
Will you sing with me this song?
I love, I love the Lord
I love, I love the Lord

He paid all the debts I could not pay
He paid all the debts I could not pay
I love, I love the Lord
I love, I love the Lord

He is a God that cannot fail
He is a God that cannot fail
I love, I love the Lord
I love, I love the Lord

He hates sin and love sinners
He hates sin and love sinners
I love, I love the Lord
I love, I love the Lord

He is the way, the truth and life
He is the way, the truth and life
I love, I love the Lord
I love, I love the Lord

Song 156

THE NAME JESUS

Give him glory, give Him honour
Salute Him King of kings
Salute Him King of kings

His kingdom will have no end
His kingdom will have no end
The name Jesus will never fail
The name Jesus will never fail
Salute Him God of Gods

He has me and you in His hands
He has me and you in His hands
His eyes are so kind and beautiful
His eyes are so kind and beautiful
Salute King of kings.

Song 157

YOUR FAITHFULNESS

Thank you for your faithfulness Jesus
Thank you for your faithfulness Jesus
You are really a faithful God
You are really a faithful God

Even when I am not faithful
You are faithful to me
You are really a faithful God

Even though I sing from now till tomorrow
Even though I sing from now till eternity
Jesus I cannot thank you enough for your faithfulness
You are really a faithful God

Song 158

JUST CALL UPON THE NAME

Just call upon the name, Just call upon the name
Just call upon the name of Jesus
There is power in the name of Jesus
The name of Jesus has power to set you free from bondage
The name of Jesus has power to destroy the work of Satan

There is healing in the name of Jesus
There is freedom in the name of Jesus
Everything you need is in the name of Jesus
Everything you need is in the name of Jesus
Hope in the name of Jesus
Peace in the name of Jesus

Song 159

JESUS IS WORTHY

Jesus is worthy, oh my King is worthy
Jesus us worthy He is to be praised, He is worthy to be praised.
Angeles bow and worship Him, they shout hallelujah,
They lift Him higher, the Lamb who was slain.
Oh I will bow and worship Him, I will shout Hallelujah
I will lift Him higher, the Lamb who was slain.
Come on bow and worship Him, come on shout hallelujah
Lift Jesus higher, the Lamb who was slain.
Oh Jesus is worthy, oh my King is worthy,
Jesus is worthy, is worthy to be praised.

ON THE DAY I WILL SEE JESUS

On the day I will see Jesus, the humble King, who died for me
I will lay prostrate before Him, I will praise Him, I will praise Him
I will praise Him, on that day when I see Him face to face
Oh that day is coming and it is coming soon
Jesus will come as His disciples saw Him going
He will come in His glory, He will come in His glory
And those who believed in Him, shall shout hallelujah, shall shout hallelujah
We are going home.
Sometimes I wonder, sometimes I wonder how the King of kings face to face.
Shake His hands, shake His hands, to see the face of Jesus everyday
Oh Jesus, Jesus, Jesus, I really want come where you are, Jesus
I really want come where you are, Jesus, I want to live you forever
really want to come where you are Jesus, I want to live with you forever
I want to behold your glory, I want behold your beauty
I want to behold you my King, I want to see you every day
Wonderful Jesus, precious King of kings, I will worship you
I will worship you, I will sing holy, holy, I will sing holy, holy, everyday.

Song 160

A SONG OF FORGIVENESS

In the pool of your blood, which you shed for me
In the pool of your blood, which you shed for me
Dip me in, Dip me in
Wash me clean Jesus, Wash me clean
In the pool of your blood
Forgive me, forgive me
Oh Lord have mercy on me
Oh Lord have mercy on me

My sins are many before you
My sins are many before you
Jesus has mercy on me
I repent all my sins Jesus
I repent all my sins
Have mercy on me

Write my name in the book of life
Write my name in the book of life
Jesus has mercy on me
Write my name in the book of life
Write my name in the book of life
Have mercy on me

Song 161

ALMIGHTY GOD

Almighty God, Almighty God
You are beautiful Majesty
You are wonderful Majesty

Your highness, I love you
Your highness, I praise you
Your highness, I bless you
Your highness, I thank you

Your majesty,
You are worthy Lord
You are worthy Lord
You are worthy Lord, King Jesus
Your majesty,

You are my defender you are my helper
You are my fighter only you
You are my shield, I love you
Your majesty,
You are merciful, you are patient Jesus
Your majesty, I praise you

Song 162

DEPEND ON YOU

Oh Jesus, Oh Jesus
I depend on you
I rely on you, I lean on you, I hope in you
Only you Lord

You are my shelter, you are my refuge
You are my healer, Oh Lord
Without you Jesus, I know I am lost
Without you Jesus, I can't find anything
Because I know Jesus, nothing is too big for you
Oh Jesus you do everything
Because I know Jesus, nothing is too hard for you
Oh Jesus you know everything

Song 163

BEGINNING AND END

Beginning and end, I worship you
Beginning and end, I worship you
Beginning and end

Beginning and end
I worship you

Lion of Judah, I worship you
God Almighty, I worship you
Beginning and end
Beginning and end
I worship you

I fall at your feet Jesus
I fall at your feet Jesus
I bow and worship you
I bow and worship you
Beginning and end
Beginning and end
I worship you

You are powerful and mighty
You are powerful and mighty
You are lifted higher Jesus
You are lifted higher Jesus
Beginning and end
Beginning and end
I worship you.

Song 164

JEHOVAH DEFENDER

We worship you, we worship you
We worship you oh Majesty
We worship you oh Majesty
Great I am we worship you
King of Kings, we worship you
I am that I am we adore you
We worship you oh Majesty

Jehovah provider, we worship you

Jehovah defender, we worship you
Jehovah our giver, we worship you
We worship you oh Majesty

You are so sweet and beautiful
You are the flower that never fades
Your beauty is undeniable
We worship you oh majesty

Song 165

NO OTHER GOD

Be lifted higher Jesus
Be lifted higher Jesus, higher above higher
There is no other God except you
There is no other God except you

You walk with me in the fire
You walk with me in the fire
There is no other God except you
There is no other God except you

In the ocean you are with me
In the ocean you are with me
You promised to never leave me
There is no other God except you
There is no other God except you

Who can keep me Jesus like you?
Who can guide me Jesus like you?
Who can died for me? But you
There is no other God except you
There is no other God except you

Song 166

FULL OF GLORY

Oh Lord I praise you, Oh Lord I praise you
Oh Lord I praise you
Lamb of God, seated upon the throne
King of kings, seated upon the throne
You reign by power and mighty
Oh Lord I praise you

You are dressed in majesty
Clothed in honour, you are full of glory
Oh Lord I praise you

Great I am all sufficient God
You supply all my needs
Oh Lord I praise you

Consuming fire, merciful God
Full of patience, Oh Lord I praise you

Song 167

I FOUND LOVE

I found love, I found love
I found love real sweet love in Jesus
I have never found love like this in my life
His love is so sweet, so different
Sweet love of love

I searched for a long time, looking for love like this
I have never found love like Jesus' love in my life
I am in love with the king of kings
I am in love with the king of kings
Jesus loves me, I love him
I fell in love with Jesus

I fell in love with Jesus
I fell in love with Jesus
He is the only one who can love me for who I am no matter what
He can never complain about me
He is so understanding, real love sweet love of Jesus
Real love, sweet love of Jesus.

Song 168

JESUS WILL NEVER FORSAKE ME

Jesus will never forsake me
Jesus will never leave me, I am standing on the promises on the of Jesus
I am counting every good promise that He has promised
because I know, He will never lie to me
I am standing on the word of Jesus

Yes I am standing on the word of Jesus
The word of Jesus is my solid rock
Even if wind blows
I know where I will go, I know where I will hide
I know Jesus will hide me

I will never be moved, I will never be shaken
Because you are my hiding place
You are my hiding place
My refuge, my tower, my help
If I call Jesus, let me tell you He will answer me
I know He will answer me
Jesus has promised never to leave me

Song 169

AN INVITATION TO THE MARRIAGE SUPPER OF THE LAMB

Blessed are those who are called to the marriage supper of the Lamb
Blessed are those who are called to the marriage supper of the Lamb

There will be singing
There will be dancing
There will be no worries
There will be no worries
Blessed are those who are called to the marriage supper of the Lamb
We will be rejoicing
We will be eating with Jesus
What a wonderful time? In the presence of the Lord
What a wonderful time? In the presence of the Lord

We will sing forever, will dance forever
We will laugh forever, our God almighty reigns

Invitations are still on going
You are invited; you are invited to the marriage supper of the Lamb

Everybody get ready, everybody get ready
The bride-groom is coming; the bride-groom is coming
And is coming very, very soon

Everybody get ready, everybody set go
Everybody set go, the table must be full
The table of Jesus must be full
The table of Jesus must be full
The bride groom is coming to give each and everyone according to what we have done
His table must be full, His table must be full

Are you one of His invited guests?
Are you one of His invited guests?

Say yes, I am one of His invited guest
Say yes, I am one of His invited guest
To the marriage supper of the Lamb
Everybody get ready, everybody set go
We are going; we are going to meet our bride-groom in air, to meet our bride-groom in air
Come on everybody must go
We will go, no one must be left

We will go, no one must be left
To the marriage supper of the Lamb

We are coming, we are coming
We are ready; we are ready to meet our bride-groom in air
To meet our bride-groom in air

We shall shout hallelujah
We shall shout hallelujah
Our bride-groom has come
Our bride-groom has come

His table must be full his table must be full
Jesus is coming, He is coming I know
Jesus is coming, He is coming I know
My friend you are going to meet our bride-groom in air
My brother you are going to meet our bride-groom in air
My sister you are going to meet our bride-groom in air
Blessed are those who are called to the marriage supper of the lamb

Song 170

LOOK IN HEAVEN

Jesus is coming; Jesus is coming back for you and me
Think about everything in heaven
A place where you will never be hungry in heaven
A place where you will never be thirsty in heaven
A place where you will never weep in heaven
Jesus has everything for you in heaven

Angels will be your waiters in heaven
You will eat with Jesus in heaven
Jesus has everything for you in heaven

It doesn't matter what you are going through right now
Lift your eyes and look in heaven
Jesus has everything for you in heaven

Song 171

HE WANTS TO DINE WITH YOU

Jesus is standing at your door
He is knocking will you let Him come in?
Will you let Him come in?
He wants to dine with you.
Jesus wants to dine with you.
He wants to dine with you.
Will you let him come in?
Will you let him come in?
Will you let him come in?

This song is a prayer that I prayed for England after I have opened my letter and found that home office had sent me three hundred eight pounds. When they asked me to claim asylum, they started giving me money to leave on, though they gave us a house in a place very far from London, but then I was told that if get my own accommodation they will continue to give us weekly support. Then my friend, Mrs. Mary Ashfield, may God be with her always.

called her friend and asked him if we could stay in his house! He allowed us. We were in his house until our Visa came and every Monday I would go to post office to get money, whenever I get money in my hands, I would say God bless this country. One day, I was sitting at the staircase then the postman came, when I opened my letter it was money again, because I thought sine they have granted us Visa they will not give us more money leave on. When I saw it, I was speechless. I knelt down and began to sing. As I knelt down, and asked God, to receive my prayer As I prayed for the land of UK, I humbly bow on my knees, answer me oh Lord, bless and heal this Land. United Kingdom may God almighty protect you always.

May God protect you day and night, protect you from the evil one, may you be covered with the blood of Jesus.

God bless our queen and other kings to come. God keep our queen and other Kings to come, Lord God who gives wisdom to kings, let your wisdom rule in our queen.

Amen.